HOW THE GAA
SURVIVED THE TROUBLES

DESMOND FAHY was born in Omagh, County Tyrone, in 1969. He now lives in Belfast with Paula, Lorcán and Mack. This is his first book.

For Paula

ACKNOWLEDGEMENTS

Thank you to everyone who gave so freely of their time to be interviewed. Your dignity in the face of some terrible pain was humbling. Thanks also to Niall Murphy in Belfast and Brendan McCarthy in Ballycran — true clubmen. To Mummy for all her support, even when I didn't make that Rice Cup team. To Drumragh GFC for giving me the chance to realise I would never play for Tyrone. To Joe Brolly for his enthusiasm and the use of his printer. To Barry O'Donnell for his help with photographs. To *Lost Lives* for showing the way. To Malachy Logan at *The Irish Times* for giving me my first chance. To everyone at Wolfhound for giving me another one. To Paula for her unswerving encouragement and love. And to Lorcán for making me laugh. May that never stop.

How the GAA Survived the Troubles

Desmond Fahy

WOLFHOUND PRESS

First published in 2001 by
Wolfhound Press Ltd
68 Mountjoy Square
Dublin 1, Ireland
Tel: (353-1) 874 0354
Fax: (353-1) 872 0207

© 2001 Desmond Fahy

All rights reserved. No part of this book may be reproduced or utilised in any form or by any means digital, electronic or mechanical including photography, filming, video recording, photocopying, or by any information storage and retrieval system or shall not, by way of trade or otherwise, be lent, resold or otherwise circulated in any form of binding or cover other than that in which it is published without prior permission in writing from the publisher.

British Library Cataloguing in Publication Data
A catalogue record for this book is available from the British Library.

ISBN 0-86327-854-X

10 9 8 7 6 5 4 3 2 1

Front Cover Photo: Pacemaker
Cover Design: Wolfhound Press
Typeset in Century Schoolbook by Wolfhound Press
Printed and bound in Spain by GraphyCems

Contents

Chapter One: Together   7

Chapter Two: Venturing Out   9

Chapter Three: On the Edge of Everything   17

Chapter Four: A Good Son   40

Chapter Five: What Might Have Been   62

Chapter Six: The Field   87

Chapter Seven: Outposts   109

Chapter Eight: Handing on the Torch   130

Chapter Nine: Journey's End   151

Chapter One: Together

19 August 1998. A cold day for the middle of August. We had been to another funeral in Beragh that morning and when we arrived at the parish church in Drumquin we had to stand outside in the mizzling rain because there were already so many people crammed inside. As echoed snatches of Philomena Skelton's funeral mass drifted from the makeshift tannoy through the late-summer Tyrone air, we stood together in small clusters and made uneasy, half-whispered small talk.

This was GAA country and this was unmistakably a GAA funeral. To almost everyone involved in the games within the county Kevin Skelton was known both as a respected referee and as a long-serving administrator. On this August afternoon he had come with his children to the chapel just a few hundred yards from the family home to bury his wife, Philomena.

Just four days before, they had made the short nine-mile journey to Omagh. The annual school-uniform shopping trip had become a family ritual. Some time after three o'clock that Saturday afternoon, as they discussed the whys and wherefores of what they needed, Kevin drifted away from Kells' drapery shop and wandered into the hardware shop next door. Minutes later, the Real IRA bomb went off. Kevin was unhurt but Philomena was already dead when he went back to find her; their daughter Shauna had been badly injured.

Now they had taken Philomena back to Drumquin to bury her. Half an hour after the funeral mass had begun, small pockets of young boys and girls, aged maybe 12 or 13, appeared outside the main door of the chapel. Some wore tracksuit tops, others football jerseys, all in the maroon and white colours of the local Drumquin Wolfe Tones GAA club. The members of this makeshift guard of honour stood around talking quietly to one another and looking just a little embarrassed, self-conscious and unsure about what exactly they were supposed to be doing.

Then one or two officials from the club gathered them together and issued their instructions in hushed voices. A few minutes later the children positioned themselves on either side of the path which wound down from the chapel towards the road below. By now the rain had eased but a biting wind had taken its place. Every now and again some of the girls who were wearing football shorts gave small, involuntary shivers.

As the funeral mass ended, hundreds of people streamed out through the chapel doors. They crowded around each other, almost huddling for warmth or comfort — or both. The eaves of the chapel roof protected some of the crowd from the wind but many more were left to stand around on the grass. The pallbearers and Philomena Skelton's coffin emerged painfully slowly from the gloom of the chapel and into the daylight. The boys and girls in the guard of honour bowed their heads.

In the graveyard almost opposite the Skelton family home there were many familiar faces. There were the grown-up faces of the boys who had been opponents in the under-age football games we used to trek off to on Tuesday nights and wintry Saturday mornings. There were referees — men like Kevin Skelton, who had presided over our first, inept steps down the GAA road all those years ago. There were the team managers and the mentors, without whom the GAA would never have become the life-force it now was — men and women from a lifetime steeped in these games in this small northern corner of the GAA world. After this they might never be quite the same again.

When it was all over, we stood together again in the nearby parish hall, eating sandwiches and cake, and drinking milky cups of tea from china cups. And for those few minutes we had never in our entire lives felt closer or more like GAA people.

Chapter Two: Venturing Out

It must have been in late 1979. Or maybe the early part of 1980. No matter. The important thing is that when the big Saturday morning arrived we were ready. I was 10, my brother a year younger, and together we were about to start our GAA journey. We had already been to a few games and watched some matches on television but this was different — this was the real thing. We were going to be Gaelic footballers.

Drumragh under-12s. It all sounded so glamorous, so grown-up. After years of aimless kick-arounds, this was real, organised football. And we had been chosen to be part of it. Even the name sounded great: Drumragh GFC — better than anything we had made up ourselves in the garden. After years of self-sufficiency this was something to belong to. It was something that would be ours. This was the GAA. This was the big time.

It's hard now to remember how it all started. The club had been formed only a few years before and it was clearly anxious to recruit young players. Why else would hopeless novices like us have been asked? It had to be pure, unadulterated desperation. But we didn't care. This was going to be our team. We were going to be Drumragh boys.

The arrangements for Saturday morning had been passed around at school a few days before. Training — the word sounded so mature — would be at 10 o'clock in St Patrick's Park in Omagh and we would be picked up some time before then. That was even better — we were going to travel together as a proper team and not have to rely on the vagaries of parental transport. Welcome to the big time!

We were up early and tried to pass the time flitting excitedly around the house. The bags were packed, unpacked and repacked. Our football gear didn't amount to much — just shorts, socks and a T-shirt. The green and white Drumragh shirt would come much later. But then there was my pride and joy — a pair of Blackthorn boots that had been polished the night before. They were clumsy, ugly things, sturdy enough to mine coal in. But that didn't matter. They were my football boots. All mine.

Some time before 10, Paddy Mullan's car swung into the yard at the back of our house. He was late; in the years to come we would discover that he was always late. We were nearest to the town, so ours was the last pick-up point. By the time it reached us, Paddy's car was already full with maybe six young bodies crammed into the back and two more in the front. But we squeezed in somehow, wedging our bags between our knees. The future stretched out in front of us. We were on our way.

*

We had grown up with Gaelic football: meaningless National League games on freezing Sunday afternoons in November; big Ulster championship occasions on sunnier days in Clones; bad-tempered club matches all over Tyrone. It was a living, breathing part of our lives, much more real than the English football matches we watched on television on Saturday nights and Sunday afternoons. Gaelic football was our game and from a very early stage we were GAA people.

The All-Ireland final at the end of September was always a big occasion. The front room would be prepared like a cinema, with the curtains closed and every available chair crowded around the television. The picture from RTÉ was never good so everyone had to get as close as possible to see what was happening. And just like at the cinema, the cardinal rule was that there was to be absolutely no talking during the main feature.

Like many Catholics at the time in Northern Ireland, we always looked south to the Republic for our news and information. The pattern was established because broadcasters in Belfast all but ignored the GAA and we relied on RTÉ in Dublin for coverage and results; over time this extended to current affairs as well. If there was to be any culture in our lives, it was GAA culture and it was Irish culture.

The impact of those early, shaping influences may have faded over time but it has never gone away. As Northern Catholics we were never in any doubt about our innate Irishness and our allegiances to that vague, unshaped ideal. There were no other cultural reference points to which we could attach ourselves in that closed world of mid-Troubles Northern Ireland. It was sink or swim.

The GAA was like a life buoy and we clung on doggedly. These were days of almost total self-reliance; anything the GAA got, it got for itself. All across Northern Ireland small groups of dedicated men spent their Saturday mornings and their weekday evenings driving young boys to training sessions and preparing teams for matches. Drumragh GFC was no different from all the rest. These volunteers watched as we splashed and slid through the mud and the puddles in games that bore only a passing resemblance to Gaelic football. They took us on trips to places like Kerry and Galway where we were beaten in challenge matches during the day and played at being men at night. They laughed as we shivered in the showers at St Patrick's Park — the water was always chilled to absolute perfection.

The truth is that if those men hadn't given so much of themselves in these ways, there was nobody else to bother. They were responsible for the nurturing of an entire GAA generation and for ensuring the survival of the Association at a time when its very existence appeared under threat. Their commitment was important because it went beyond the creation of an environment for shapeless games of under-age football. It showed that the GAA could provide a cultural outlet that was both non-threatening and non-violent, and it allowed a significant proportion of the Northern Irish population to keep in touch with itself.

All of this was reinforced in the schools. Twenty years ago vocations were still sufficiently strong to ensure that Catholic schools still had priests and brothers on their staffs. Although the point was seldom, if ever, made overtly, the underlying tone of the education they provided was resolutely Irish and nationalist. Gaelic games played a central part in this.

At primary school, the summit of sporting achievement was to win a place on the Rice Cup team; the Rice Cup was a Gaelic football competition for the older boys. Most of us fell some way short of making the team. But the importance of the games and the cultural statement we were making by being part of them was very much part of the fabric of school life.

This continued into secondary level where the Christian Brothers took over in earnest. The teaching of Irish was a core element of the curriculum and the playing of football and hurling went in tandem with that. Hurling, in particular, survived in many parts of Northern Ireland thanks only to the evangelical zeal of Brothers from the game's hotbeds of Cork and Kilkenny. More often than not, they must have wondered why they were bothering as they stood on the sideline watching our hopeless attempts to master the game's finer and more subtle skills. But still they kept coming back for more, and we kept listening. Together we were GAA people.

Politics impinged very little on our lives. We were vaguely aware of the murders and the bombings but, in reality, we were totally detached from them. They were the terrible things that happened in cities like Belfast and Derry — not in small, quiet towns like Omagh. Or so we thought. But even in our closeted GAA lives we had inklings that we were different. We could watch soccer on television, but we were not allowed to play. We supported the Ireland rugby team when it played England, but the game was never played at our school. Cultural confusion was there right from the beginning.

To be a member of the GAA was to feel different and set slightly apart. We realised that much, but we had no idea of the ill-feeling, antagonism and even outright hatred the mere fact of that involvement could provoke in other people. We didn't know that you could be attacked on the streets of your own town if you were carrying a hurling stick or the wrong sports bag. We didn't know that the state could take over your football field and there wasn't a single thing you could do about it. We didn't know that people would come at night and try to burn down GAA dressing rooms and halls. We didn't know that men could be abducted from outside their own GAA clubs and shot dead. We would find these things out later.

Bit by bit those feelings of difference seeped into our lives and the questions started to emerge. If the GAA was the influential sporting and cultural influence we thought it was, why was it never on the television? If it performed such an important function in providing activity for hundreds upon hundreds of children, why did it receive no public funding, and why did clubs like ours rely on sponsored walks to raise money for jerseys and footballs? Why were we made to feel so isolated? There were more questions than answers.

And so it went on, this very Northern Irish form of cultural and sporting apartheid. The rules were well-rehearsed and the boundaries well-recognised, and there is no reason to suspect that the status quo would not have persisted for another generation. But a change had to come from somewhere and that arrived with the IRA hunger strikes of 1981.

*

As one death followed another through the spring and the summer of 1981 the nationalist protests against British government policy mushroomed. In many cases they were protests without a real focal point, and that is where the GAA clubs, reluctantly, became involved. Some of the men who died, like Kevin Lynch from Dungiven, had been active members of the Association and so it became inevitable that the clubs themselves would respond. After each hunger striker died, sympathy notices from clubs all over Northern Ireland would be scattered through the death notices of the local newspapers. Whether it liked it or not, the GAA was being linked in the wider public arena to the hunger strikes and to the general discontent that surrounded them.

This was a difficult time. Throughout the Troubles up to that point, the GAA had stuck rigidly to its avowedly non-political stance, and had refused to descend from there into the lowlands of day-to-day Northern Ireland politics. Its broad nationalist agenda was no secret, but the Association did its best to prevent that agenda from being given a political dimension. The overriding concern was that any shift at all in this position could result in the GAA's becoming drawn into the unfolding conflict. That, in turn, would have had catastrophic consequences for a membership which already felt under concerted and persistent threat in Northern Ireland.

Somehow the GAA hierarchy in Ulster managed to hold the line. But only just. It was a perilous balancing act meeting the demands for action and protest from the members on the ground, while at the same time working to prevent the Association as a whole from getting sucked into the trench warfare of the political crisis. It was a situation that required men of integrity and vision; they did the best they could.

However, after the hunger strikes the GAA could never be the same again. The exigencies of the situation in Northern Ireland now made it abundantly clear that the days of a naïve GAA policy of total disengagement were gone for ever. The hunger strikes changed the GAA because they showed it that no body with its cultural clout and its sporting dominance could remain totally aloof from politics. The history of the GAA in Northern Ireland in the twenty years since then has seen the Association searching, with varying degrees of success, for some workable definition of what its political role might be.

Once this process of evolution had begun, there was no turning back, no way that a finger could suddenly be jammed into the dyke. The GAA was changing and those changes were also shaping us. The organisation gradually became more confident about itself and about its place in the society around it. There was a new stridency to the way it went about its business and positioned itself. The GAA had become something to be proud of and something to celebrate. It was striding in from the margins and pulling us along with it.

The media profile of the Association increased ten-fold as broadcasters belatedly gave football and hurling some recognition and air-time. Just a few years before, the Ulster championship had been all but ignored by the mainstream media. By the start of the 1990s rival local television channels were fighting bitterly over the rights to show the games. It was a radical and dramatic transformation but it was an indication of the distance the GAA and its people had travelled in a remarkably short time.

This enhanced public profile, however, came at a considerable price. The old hegemony was being challenged as the long-time outsiders were brought in from the cold. But the old antipathy directed towards the GAA had not gone away. If anything, it had hardened and had taken on more sinister and malevolent forms. The 1990s may have been a golden age for the GAA in Northern Ireland, but they were also a period when its members came under sustained, often murderous, attack.

The overall death toll may have been diminishing dramatically as the long haul towards peace trundled on, but the number of attacks directed against the GAA and its membership was increasing, as was the severity of these attacks. The murders of Seán Brown and Gerry Devlin were the most obvious examples of this. They occurred against a backdrop of arson, criminal damage and intimidation directed against the clubs, particularly in rural areas.

Such attacks politicised the GAA to an extent that would not have seemed possible just a decade before, but the embracing of that political dimension became an essential part of the organisation's survival strategy. The GAA had moved into the mainstream and was discovering the influence it could exert there. But with that influence came both responsibility and criticism.

Most pertinently, the Association spent most of the 1990s defending its retention of Rule 21, which prohibits members of the security forces from being GAA members. This rule yoked the GAA to the most contentious issue of the entire peace process — that of policing — and ensured that the political spotlight would continue to be shone in its direction. The ongoing Rule 21 debate has coloured the GAA's public image and, on more than one occasion, has been used as a stick with which to beat the Association.

The way in which policy towards it has developed — first ignoring it completely, then trying to remove it with undue haste, and eventually settling on a commitment to abolish when the time is right — provides an insight into the workings of the GAA. With swings from ramshackle to highly principled and back again, it seems as if lessons from the past go unlearnt for an alarmingly long period of time.

Nevertheless, one event — the Real IRA bombing of Omagh in August 1998 — towers over this period. Its effect on Northern Irish society as a whole was traumatic and cataclysmic. The GAA itself lost members — young members — with many more injured and scarred by the experience. Omagh represented for the GAA the biggest single challenge of the Troubles, and there were times when it appeared genuinely bereft of ideas as to how it might cope and respond. But true to the recurring motif of this entire period, the GAA got through it. The process was a troubled and tortuous one, but the Association survived and emerged on the other side a stronger, more confident organisation.

Somehow we all survived; we all got through it. The journey that began that first morning as we waited for Paddy Mullan's car has encompassed laughter, friendship, fear and mourning. But most of all it has been a journey through GAA land. Together we are living GAA lives and we have been immeasurably enriched by the entire experience.

*

On a muggy September afternoon we have the blinds drawn and chairs arranged around the television in the corner. It is just as if the intervening twenty years have never happened. Armagh are playing Kerry in an All-Ireland semi-final replay; my 16-month old son wanders unsteadily in and out of the room, wearing an Armagh replica shirt which is at least two sizes too big for him. Every now and then he catches sight of the football and shouts excitedly at the screen. Another journey is beginning.

Chapter Three: On the Edge of Everything

It is May Day in Belfast. The coolness of the morning is a lingering sign that spring is still hanging around, but as the sunshine hesitantly nudges through, summer feels just a breath or two away. All that is needed now is some gentle cajoling.

At the St Enda's club in north Belfast they're ready for the change in the seasons. A fast-food truck parked just beside the club house has doubled up as an ice-cream van and is doing good business. Up here, right on the edge of the city, the wind can cut through you on icy, winter afternoons, but today it's T-shirt-and-shorts weather.

There are children everywhere. Some are kicking footballs up and down the side of the field. Down below on the training pitch seven or eight of them have organised an impromptu game of their own. Their shouts and the noise of their quickly forgotten disputes travel quickly across the wide open spaces. Anticipation of the care-free, school-free months that are just around the corner hangs in the air.

Out on the full pitch a hurling game is in progress. Today is the day when St Enda's hosts the Seán Fox Memorial Shield, a football competition for clubs within Belfast city; the hurling game is the supporting act. The thirty boys cannot be more than 11 or 12 years old, and the full expanse of the field seems to dwarf them. In the middle, a referee tries to keep some sort of order, but a wonderful, light-hearted atmosphere prevails. The enjoyment of the game is all that matters.

One side wears shirts, the other wears none, and the boys pull, hook and run around with unquenchable enthusiasm. The one or two players who are operating on a higher level stand out immediately; time and again they leave everyone else trailing in their weaving wake. They will play on bigger stages in the future, but this is not a game that is about winning or losing.

The real achievement and the true worth of the occasion is what it says about the rude health of this club and the way in which it is confidently facing into the future. *Mol an óige is tiocfaidh sí.* Praise the youth and they will come. St Enda's should not have many problems in the months and years ahead. But there were many darker days when celebratory events like this seemed a lifetime away.

*

When the first people moved up here over forty years ago Glengormley was as far north as you could go in Belfast before you found yourself in the rolling countryside of south Antrim. It was one of the new suburbs, and for those who had lived their lives in the cramped, squeezed-together streets of the west and north of the city it offered the possibility of better housing and some space to bring up a family.

Many jumped at the opportunity and made the move. The area also attracted the first generation of people from the country who came to the city looking for work. The fact that the fields and the relative calm of the countryside were just a few miles north softened the blow of adjusting to city life. Some of the families who arrived in the new surroundings had already been steeped in the GAA down in the city; so they brought it with them.

Glengormley was one of the few places in Belfast where town met country head on. At first, common ground was not that easy to find, but within a short time it became clear that the GAA was going to serve as the glue that would bind this new community together. Seán Fox had grown up steeped in Irish culture and, like many others, found himself, almost by accident, living and bringing up a family in Glengormley. His son, Dermot, remembers:

> My father was an Irish-language speaker from he was very young. He always worked his whole life to promote the Irish language. He actually came from the Falls Road originally but ended up here because he worked for a fish firm called T Keenan and Son who opened a shop in Glengormley and he was offered management of it. That's how we ended up in Glengormley and from when he arrived here he always tried to carry on what he always believed in — the promotion of the Irish language, of Irish games and of Irish culture. Obviously the club was an opportunity for him to fulfil that ambition.

Without Seán Fox and a few others like him, there would have been no St Enda's GAA club. The first germ of an idea came in the early 1950s, and Seán worked with men like Paddy Lavery and families like the Devlins to see a club formed in 1953, although it was 1956 before any teams were entered in competition. There is no great wonder that the minds of these new arrivals should eventually turn to the GAA. Without its influence in their lives, they felt that there was something missing. Starting a club was the only way they knew to fill that void.

Right from the start, the new club had to struggle against geographical imperatives. Before the influx of Catholics during the 1950s, this part of north Belfast had been predominantly Protestant. Unionist culture, in the form of band parades and Orange marches, struck the dominant cultural note. That hegemony went largely unthreatened for a generation. There were pockets of GAA activity but those involved opted for pragmatism and kept themselves to themselves. It was a different time and life was easier that way.

The arrival in Glengormley of a significant minority Catholic population, and expressions of that group's cultural identity in the form of a GAA club, represented a challenge to the status quo. The dynamics of the opposition between the two cultural groupings was to shape life in Glengormley for a generation.

'I can assure you that right from the start this club was seen as a serious threat to the status quo in Glengormley and as a result was constantly attacked,' says Dermot Fox. 'It was always perceived in this area as being a threat.'

This perception was fuelled in large part by the vibrant cultural life that soon grew up around the club, inspired by Seán Fox and a few others. Football and hurling provided obvious sporting outlets, but in a society which, at that time, paid little or no attention to nationalist culture, St Enda's became a focus for all sorts of activities. The GAA club became the cultural touchstone for this new community and played a prominent role in shaping it during those early years.

Irish language classes were the most prominent non-sporting activity of the club, and Seán Fox was the most enthusiastic proponent of the language. He spent night after night in the old clubhouse giving Irish classes to anyone in the club who was keen to learn. As political life in Northern Ireland became ever more polarised, so activities like these classes and the Gaelic games themselves tended to have an isolating effect on those who participated in them. But Seán Fox was one of those who was determined to do his bit to swim against that tide. According to his son:

> The club was a cultural outlet and a focal point for everything that went on here and all expressions of Irishness. The club had no politics at all and it always strove very, very hard to make sure that politics didn't enter into it and everybody was made equally welcome. Protestants and everybody, they were all welcome in this club. I would have to say that and I haven't been around Glengormley for 30 years because even when I was here it was a place of entertainment and a place to play Gaelic football and hurling.

During the early years there was always tension within the area as the club became increasingly confident and visible within the Catholic community in Glengormley. Numbers were also growing as more and more families made the move out of the city. Each wave of new people brought with it new tranches of GAA aficionados. Every little helped. But with this expansion came more attention from malevolent outside forces. The onset of the Troubles was the catalyst which transformed the existing mistrust and suspicion into outright antipathy and violence.

The experiences of St Enda's through the early part of the 1970s read more like a military briefing than a sporting history. In February 1972 a blast incendiary bomb was thrown onto the roof, and the clubrooms were sprayed with machine-gun fire. No one was injured but the building was burnt to the ground.

By August of the same year, St Enda's had been rebuilt only to be destroyed by another bomb. After a third bomb attack in June 1973 the decision was taken not to attempt to rebuild for another ten years. In the early part of 1974 a bomb was found in the changing rooms as players and officials were getting ready for a game. Again there were no injuries.

Throughout all of this, the struggle went on to hold the club together. Seán Fox played his part in this struggle, and fond stories about him tumble out in any conversation about the St Enda's club. One of the favourite stories concerns an incident back in the 1980s when Seán was presiding over some official event or other at the clubrooms — nobody's quite sure what the event was.

Seán was playing the role of MC and, at the appointed time, as the Irish tricolour was being hoisted up the flagpole, he gave the signal for whoever was operating the PA to start the national anthem. Twenty or thirty seconds of silence passed and it became apparent that there wasn't going to be any music.

Totally unfazed, Seán belted the anthem out himself, unaccompanied, and the flag was duly serenaded.

Needless to say, within half an hour of Seán's rendition of 'Amhrán na bhFiann', an RUC patrol had arrived at the club to order that the flag be taken down because there had been complaints from nearby residents that it was causing offence. That was how it was in parts of Belfast then and that is how life was for GAA members. A people set apart.

Nevertheless, St Enda's endured — prospered even — as its football and hurling teams gained a foothold within the Antrim leagues and championships. Seán Fox began to play a less active role, but the club hadn't forgotten what he had done for it. Others may have taken up the challenge but Seán's position as one of the founding, driving influences was to be preserved. He was made honorary President, and his continued involvement was regarded as a calm hand on the tiller.

The club, however, had not been able to fade out of the limelight as easily as its founding member. As the Troubles entered another murderous phase during the early part of the 1990s, St Enda's again came under attack. This time it was more sinister, as the focus of attacks switched from arson to murder. The first indication of this shift came in December 1992. A three-man UFF gang had arrived at the club to carry out a gun attack but was disturbed by a group of people who had decided to leave early. Instead of carrying out the attack on those attending the quiz night inside the building, the gang opened fire on the car of the departing members, injuring one of the women inside.

On 25 October 1993, St Enda's was again targeted, this time with a far more devastating effect. Seán Fox, now aged 72, was at his home in Harmin Park, Glengormley, a short distance from the football field. A group of men entered his house during the night and held him captive for an hour before shooting him. The UVF claimed responsibility with a telephone call to a Belfast newsroom. The club and the surrounding community were rocked to their foundations. Dermot Fox recalls:

> Men like my father were individuals who took their lives in their hands to promote the Irish games. They really did, because their lives and their families' lives were at risk simply because they were involved. Before my father was shot his name was put on the wall: 'Fox You're Next'. The reason being that it was an obvious tactic the way they picked individuals in areas who would be perceived as a threat to everybody in the area. So by shooting my father, every single Catholic and every single nationalist in this area felt threatened. It could be them next because he was an old man of 72 years.

Much of the violence of previous years had been random and indiscriminate and had cut away at the very fabric of communities. But this was something altogether more sinister. There were men who now felt under direct threat because of their involvement with their local club and, by extension, with the GAA as a whole. Members of this sporting and cultural organisation were now viewed by loyalist paramilitaries as fair game. The message was stark and uncompromising: to be a member of the GAA was to be a political target. The implications ran deep and dark.

Dermot Fox believes that it was all part of a strategy:

> I would say that it was a very controlled thing. They could have gone into a chapel any Sunday morning, which they never did. What they did do was identify individuals in areas who were seen as linchpins in the areas either for Nationalism or for the GAA or for whatever else and killed them. And that terrified everyone else in the area. It was very successful. It worked. This area was terrified.

Seán Fox's wife had been from Coalisland in County Tyrone, and it was decided that he should be buried there. Although the funeral was some 50 miles from Belfast, scores of club members and players made the journey to pay their respects to a man to whom they owed so much. The journey had its own symbolism as well — it represented the same meeting of city and country that had given St Enda's such a distinctive character.

In the years after his murder, St Enda's officials looked for a way to provide a more lasting memorial to the life of Seán Fox. Eventually it was decided that a football tournament would be set up for clubs within Belfast, to be played in his honour; the winner would be awarded the Seán Fox Memorial Shield. So, every May Day they gather at the club to celebrate his life. Members of the Fox family come too, and in doing so they retain that contact with St Enda's which their father made so much a part of their lives.

*

The Seán Fox Memorial tournament represents a connection with the collective past of the GAA in Belfast. It brings together clubs like St Enda's, Pearse's and Ardoyne Kickham's, and provides echoes of the north Belfast derby games that used to define the GAA in the city. And for this occasion a Wolfe Tone team has been formed for the day, drawn from north Belfast footballers affiliated to other clubs outside the area. It is a fitting tribute to a life filled with service to the GAA.

As Dermot Fox watches the final being played and sees all the entertainment that has been provided for the families and the children around the ground, he thinks about his father. He is watching the coming of age of the club that sprang from extremely modest beginnings. And he knows that, in all likelihood, this would not have happened without the valuable and selfless contribution made by his father. The dominant emotion he feels is pride — pride that St Enda's has come through to the other side of a dark tunnel; pride that everything that went before was not in vain. His father, he says, would have been proud as well.

> He would have, he would have. Hopefully now common sense is going to prevail from now on in the whole of the North here and people will be allowed to express their culture in the way they want to as long as it doesn't interfere with anybody else. That's how it is here today. My father would have thought that all the work, all the threats and all the suffering were worthwhile just to see this.

*

Kevin Devlin sits in an armchair in the living-room of his north Belfast house. Outside in the hall there is kit-bag with a pair of well-worn football boots wedged in at the side. A Chelsea match is on television. The sound on the set in the corner is turned down. Kevin is absent-mindedly looking at the screen but in his mind he is miles away.

All the time he is talking — talking about the way in which the history of his family has been so closely intertwined with that of the St Enda's club just a short walk away; talking about all the good times, all the hard, honest effort; talking about the pain of the loss of a brother and a friend.

The Devlin family arrived in Glengormley as part of the second wave of migration from the centre of Belfast. They brought with them an ingrained sense of the importance and value of the GAA — the celebration of that had always been part of the Devlin way. Kevin recalls:

> I can only speak say from 1971 onwards but my father was always a GAA man before that. We'd been to a lot of matches before moving up here. We had followed Antrim's under-21s in 1969 — the year they won the All-Ireland — down to Cork for their semi-final. It sounds maybe daft to people but really when you're GAA-minded you enjoy all those times. I went to a Christian Brothers school as well and that really would have put another aspect into everything in terms of Gaelic games and that kind of thing.

It was only natural that one of the first things the Devlins would do as soon as they had settled down into their new surroundings would be to gravitate towards the local GAA club. St Enda's was still a relatively young club and this injection of enthusiasm and new blood came at the perfect time. The social fabric of the whole area was changing subtly but inexorably, and the make-up of the club was an indication of that. Kevin Devlin is still talking:

> When we first came to Glengormley in the 1970s and the juvenile team was just starting to take off there weren't the housing developments there are now. We were lucky if we had maybe 15 or 16 youngsters at under 16. Up here was very much countryside at that particular time and I would say in relation to religion it would have divided up maybe 70:30, Protestants to Catholics. Now it's down to 60:40, and maybe 50:50, so there is a good catchment area as regards the GAA and plenty of support and back-up for St Enda's now.

Back in the early 1970s, however, the situation was more fluid. Nobody could be sure whether the political violence of the time would endure, and the all-enveloping tension that was to permeate the next thirty years was not yet a part of daily life. Kevin has fond memories of those much more innocent days:

> Again it might seem a bit strange but when I was coming up to the club in 1971 and 1972 to play games for the club it seemed like very happy times. We had sports days and tournaments, that kind of thing, and when we were coming up to play for the

juveniles there were maybe 15 or 16 of us altogether in the area that wanted to play Gaelic. You didn't feel threatened or anything, you just went up. We were a big family and the club started to take off when families like ours came in. They started then to field a couple of under-age teams at under-12 and under-14.

The strand that connected the new club with its country roots still ran strongly through St Enda's at that time. That level of continuity was important as the older men shepherded their sons and grandsons along.

There did seem to be a lot more older people around the club then — 50-, 60-, 70-year-old. More so than now. There was no gate, just Paddy Lavery going around with a cap and that's all the money the club would have lifted.

St Enda's provided a sporting and cultural reference point for a new, uncertain Catholic community in that part of Belfast; young boys like Kevin Devlin and his brothers gained self-confidence from that.

As youngsters we certainly felt very proud to be Irish and you made a big thing about the tricolour and that sort of thing. You felt a lot more Irish if you did play Gaelic — I certainly did when I was young — because it is an All-Ireland sport.

However, the harshness of the political situation that was rapidly unfolding and unravelling was pressing in on the club all the time. It quickly became apparent that the old value system was slipping away. The badge of identity that came as part of the GAA package was also a signifier of difference. It was a time when the GAA in Belfast began to suffer as a result of its own success; that was felt most keenly among the young rank-and-file players.

'I know I felt proud,' says Kevin Devlin, 'but you did realise that people possibly didn't like you or didn't want you and you then develop a bit of fear because of that.'

The geographical isolation of the football field and the clubrooms was a problem for St Enda's right from the start of the Troubles. Whereas now there are over 1,000 homes on either side of the Hightown Road where the club is situated, then it was all undeveloped farm land. There were no street lights and

3: On the Edge of Everything 27

no footpath on the way up to the club. The young boys walking up for training or a match soon became easily recognisable targets. That vulnerability was to endure for a generation. According to Kevin Devlin:

> If you were actually going up the road, the only place you were going to was the club. There was no way you would have just been walking around up there with hurley sticks or anything like that in the early days. No way. You would have been told by your parents or the people in charge of the team that you would be picked up and left back home. Or else you'd all meet up somewhere to get a minibus if we were going across town for matches. You certainly weren't allowed to stand on street corners or anything like that. My father took a lot of the teams. Because we were a big family he drove an estate car and there was no way he would have left anybody to walk even one or two streets.

This emphasis on personal security was to become as much a fact of GAA life at St Enda's as marking the pitch, Saturday-morning training sessions and fund-raising dances. To the outsider it might seem like the ultimate subversion of the sporting ideal, but pragmatism ruled in 1970s Belfast. People soon adjusted to the new rhythm, and Kevin Devlin's earliest memories of his journey with the club are as much about being under attack as they are about under-age heroics. It is as if much of the innocence that is so much a part of growing up in the GAA in other parts of the country was simply ripped out.

> In the early days we had an old stone house, like a chicken-house kind of thing, which we turned into a bit of a clubhouse. I remember being in it one day when I was eight or nine years of age. There were shots fired and a blast bomb left outside. We were told to hide under this big bit of wood that we used as a table-tennis table at the time. The lights went out and all I can remember is machine-gun fire right at the front door. Later my father told me that they thought most of the firing was straight over the club roof because not one bullet hit the premises. If that was the case it's obvious it was all about intimidation. They weren't out to actually kill that particular night — just intimidate.

The club and what it stood for quickly became a focal point within the local community. But despite being under considerable and persistent pressure, it managed to remain aloof from the political situation that was fermenting outside. Without some level of detachment from that — however tenuous it might be in reality — the club would have struggled to survive. Kevin Devlin remembers some hard-fought debates.

> There might have been people who would have wanted to be connected with the Republican movement and that was fair enough. But I think the fact is that St Enda's did not have any politics or allow any politics to creep into the club. There were meetings of the committee and anything that was asked for from outside the club or any requests that were made, they were always turned down. There was one particular time when they had to have a vote on it and it was decided that there was no way the club was going to have anything to do with holding any outside meetings.

The absence of any sectarian or political dimension within the fabric of St Enda's was vital; it destroyed any possible legitimacy that might be claimed for the campaign of intimidation and attack waged against it. Instead, the club functioned as a kind of pressure valve for the release of cultural tensions that might otherwise have been diverted elsewhere. St Enda's was not alone in this, of course, as GAA clubs throughout Northern Ireland struggled to keep young members away from protest and violence. But the stakes were particularly high in north Belfast at the height of the Troubles. Kevin Devlin says:

> The men on the committees during those days were great ambassadors for the games as far as I was concerned. With the time, effort and commitment they put in to try and make a club and make a team and teach the culture, they didn't have time for anything else. They weren't paramilitaries hanging around street corners or anything like that. Any spare time was spent up at St Enda's. One thing that the GAA does say to its members is that it's non-political and non-sectarian. And I have to say that I do not remember anything political or sectarian in our club over all the years I've been involved.

In the main, this was respected. There were some mixed pubs in Glengormley, and the way the St Enda's men used to gather in one corner to hold impromptu committee meetings about this team or that fund-raiser became an accepted part of life in the area. In many quarters there was clear, unequivocal respect for the GAA. But outside that enlightened consensus darker skies were gathering.

Harassment of GAA members by the security forces was widely reported. This could take the more subtle form of roadblocks outside the grounds, but could also extend to thinly veiled threats and even violence. The net effect of both was the same. GAA life was made difficult and, at times, frightening.

> The UDR when they were formed gave us a hard time. The 16-, 17- and 18-year-olds were arrested and searched every night of the week. And they would maybe drive up through the pitches and through the goals and pull the nets down with the jeeps. It probably was very dangerous in those days but people didn't maybe realise just how dangerous it really was.

By now, the Devlin family was an established fixture at the club, part of the core group of players and administrators who helped steer St Enda's through those difficult times. As the Devlins became immersed in the club, so they became immersed in the emerging Glengormley community. The club was gradually becoming strong at under-age level, and Kevin and his brother, Gerry, were making the same journey together.

> He was exactly the same as myself. He was up there at the club from no age as well — there was a year-and-a-half or so between us. The older ones in our family would have been at the GAA matches with our father in those days and so we would have been first up to the club to play in the teams.

As Gerry Devlin moved from the under-age teams to adulthood, he quickly became an important part of the senior set-up. On the football field, St Enda's was making progress, and Gerry was one of those helping to lead the charge. From an early stage he had established himself as a leader — a figure to be looked up to and respected. However, a cruciate ligament injury represented a severe set-back.

The surgery and subsequent recovery period can be daunting for professional sportsmen and women, never mind an amateur Gaelic footballer trying to keep a full-time job. But Gerry threw himself into it with characteristic perseverance and dedication.

A health-care scheme at work took care of the operation and, to help with his recuperation, Gerry had a chair specially made with a small iron bar across it. Kevin remembers going to visit his brother at the time, and while they were talking together, Gerry would be exercising his leg back and forwards over the iron bar and strengthening the torn knee muscles.

The initial prognosis had been poor but nobody was surprised when Gerry Devlin returned to football within a year. He started first with the reserves and discovered a real talent for nurturing the young talent on that side and coaxing and cajoling the best out of those around him. This was a revelation that was to serve him and St Enda's well in the future. Within another year, Gerry was back playing on the senior team. Then his football life took another twist. Kevin recalls:

> In the second match of that season, he damaged the other knee, the cruciate again, and he said to me that was it. After what he put in to get back playing in the first place, to do the other knee was just far too much for him.

However, the GAA and Gaelic football had got too close at this stage. They were so much part of him that, try as he might, Gerry Devlin was always going to be drawn back in; he just couldn't leave all that behind. So, he moved into management and took charge of the St Enda's senior side. Looking back, his brother feels that he was already ahead of his time.

> He was 26, 27 at the time, so when he did go into management it was very early. But he had started to see the way that football was changing during the 1980s and he noticed it getting a bit faster and the players getting a bit fitter. I think Gerard was one of the first to cotton on to that.

Beyond the day-to-day business of devising training schedules and plotting tactics, Gerry Devlin also uncovered a particular gift for man-management. St Enda's had traditionally been a strong hurling club but now the fortunes of a moribund football team were being radically transformed and he was right there at the heart of it all.

> I think he just knew where to draw the line with most people. Some people you can give a rollicking to, some people you

can't. We didn't win a senior championship match for three or four years but Gerry was working away and thinking about it. He got other coaches in from all over the county to take the odd session before championship matches — that had never been heard of at the club before, an outsider coming in like that. The other thing about him was he liked the 'bus run'. Before the season started we'd head off somewhere for a challenge game to build up a bit of team spirit for the coming year. Another year we did a sponsored cycle in relays to Dublin and all that sort of thing to build up spirit. That was shown then on the pitch later on.

Gerry and Kevin Devlin also realised the threat to the very future of the club that the ongoing cycle of arson and bomb attacks represented. The situation had deteriorated dramatically with the murder of Seán Fox, and the brothers could see confidence and a sense of well-being seeping away from St Enda's. They decided to act and try to set some sort of example for others to follow.

Once the decision had been made to travel to Seán Fox's funeral in Coalisland, Gerry encouraged as many of the senior footballers as he could to travel down with him. Some of the hurlers went as well, and the communal act of paying their respects bound the club together at a time when it looked like it might fall apart altogether. Looking back now, Kevin realises that that simple gesture may have saved the club from disaster.

> I remember the week after Seán Fox had died and the club was opening again. It was empty, nobody would go up. Gerard, me and another fella decided to go up one Friday night and then the Friday after that again. We kept that going for a few weeks, had our pints and just locked up early. We would never let the barman lock up on his own or anything like that. We would maybe get a lift with him and, by God, I remember standing waiting to get into the car at night after locking the gates and just waiting and waiting. Frightening times. The fear in that club at that particular time was second to none but we were just making a stand by going up those Friday nights.

By the end of 1997, Gerry Devlin had settled into his new role and his thoughts were turning to the new year and the upcoming football season. There was a lot to be optimistic about

and he had already started to put together a plan of campaign.
Off the field, St Enda's was making progress as well. The old,
much-targeted clubhouse was due to be replaced in a few months'
time by a new hall, bar and dressing-room complex. Friday,
5 December, was a special occasion and some of the St Enda's
members had decided to give the old clubhouse a good send-off.

Kevin went up on his own. The ritual was the same. A steel
door and buzzer at the gate had been fitted for security reasons
and these had to be negotiated before he got inside.

> It was planned that it would be the last weekend of the old
> clubhouse. It was one terrible night, weatherwise, I remember
> that. Gerard had been off the drink for three or four weeks at
> the time.

The plan was that Gerry would come up a bit later, maybe to
join them and to give some of them a lift home. When he
arrived, just before 11 p.m., an LVF gunman was waiting. A
short time later, Gerry Devlin's body was found by a club
member just outside the security gate. He had been shot seven
times. Kevin Devlin was one of the first people on the scene as
people came out of the club. The funeral a few days later was a
traumatic occasion and almost three years later all the grief and
loss still echo around Kevin Devlin's living-room.

> I happened to maybe scream a few words at the graveyard
> myself. I think what I said was along the lines that we would
> never be beaten and that we will open the club again and we
> will open the pitch. Those were things I felt I had to say.
> I believed them myself and I believed Gerry would have said
> that. Just to keep the club going. I was numb after all of that,
> maybe numb for a year after. I would say that the club then
> would have gone down the drain, just like that, only for the
> work of people at the club itself.

Kevin and the rest of the family struggled through the
aftermath of Gerry's murder, often finding some solace in
unlikely places. It was only in the months after his death that
Kevin began fully to understand the way in which his brother
had immersed himself so completely in their GAA club, in their
St Enda's.

He kept books when he was manager — I specifically asked for them when he died. For every match when he was in charge he kept a record, this big A4 diary. He would have had the team picked, and the subs, two days before he had the fixture highlighted in *The Irish News* and then when you flicked the page over, the result was there from the paper as well.

The attention to detail, right down the minutiae of preparing the team, was a wonderful and treasured thing for Kevin to see. There in black and white was a permanent memorial to Gerry's dedication and service to the GAA.

There was a record of all the people at training on the Wednesday, and stapled at the back he had a note of the holidays that everyone was taking so he could plan ahead. It's amazing — and don't forget he was only 30 years of age or so at the time. He was always thinking — it must have been all day, every day for him.

Gerry Devlin's murder took all that away. It also had a terrorising effect at three different levels. Firstly, the Devlin family lost a son, brother and father. Secondly, following on from the death of Seán Fox, Gerry's murder rocked the St Enda's club to its very foundations. And finally, it sent shockwaves through the entire GAA community, highlighting the members' terrible vulnerability in the face of such random violence.

Just seven months previously, Seán Brown had been murdered in south Derry; attentions now appeared to have turned towards Belfast. The inescapable implication was that no GAA member anywhere in Northern Ireland could feel totally safe. Kevin Devlin lost both a brother and a fellow GAA member, but for him the loss was essentially simply a human one.

The way I see it is that they got a good one that night. I know that maybe sounds a bit selfish but to me it made it harder for us and better for them that they got one of the good ones from the GAA in Gerry. There's nobody goes up to that club any better or less a person than anyone else but they certainly got a good one when they got Gerry. He was just a dedicated GAA man.

*

The walls of the St Enda's clubhouse are papered with all the usual posters and messages. There is news of upcoming fund-raising events, the indoor hurling league that is played during the winter, and notification of the training sessions for the senior and reserve players. St Enda's is a busy city club and its message board is just the same as those you could expect to see in GAA clubs up and down the country.

There are photographs as well, of awards presentations and team line-ups. Again, there is nothing particularly unusual in that. But one stands out. It was taken at Trench House in Belfast and is dated 12 January 1975. In fact, it could not have been taken at any other point in history. The give-aways are the standard-issue wing colours of the time, which have been grafted onto the light-coloured football shirts, and the tousled, unruly 1970s haircuts. Clothes and hairstyles clearly date young Gaelic footballers in the same way that they date everyone else.

There are twenty-two young faces in the photograph; twenty are members of the St Enda's under-12 team, and there are two mentors at either end of the back row, although they don't look much older than the players beside them. The photograph was taken on the day the side won the local league competition for that age group. Each boy's face is fresh, unlined and bursting with youthful innocence — full of enthusiasm for the future that appears to be stretching out in front of every one of them.

In other, bigger and more established clubs, this event — the winning of an under-12 league — might have gone by relatively unnoticed. But back in the mid-1970s St Enda's was only a young club, unused enough as yet to leagues or championships, so when they did come along, they were celebrated eagerly. The boys look shy and just a little awkward. It is almost as if they have been encouraged to pose under false pretences; the photographer seems to have captured them in all their slightly uncertain glory without their express permission. Some of them appear bemused — as if this photograph has caught them right in the middle of that limbo period between childhood and adolescence, and they don't like the intrusion one little bit.

As a piece of club history all of this makes the photograph significant enough. But the roll call printed underneath hammers home its importance as a valuable social document. This picture has its own stories to tell.

Among the names of the boys standing in the back row are those of Liam Canning and Gerry Devlin. They stand out from the rest because they are followed by three stark letters in blunt, black type. RIP.

Gerry Devlin must have been just over-age for this under-12 team because he is wearing a pair of flared jeans and standing guard at the left-hand side of the back row. His clothes make him look older than the boys on the team, but his face is still youthful and vulnerable. Kevin Devlin, meanwhile, is squatting in the crowded front row.

Gerry's story has been told. Liam Canning's fate is less well known.

On the morning of 9 August 1981, Liam Canning was walking along Alliance Avenue in north Belfast with his girlfriend. An off-duty UDR man in a derelict building nearby fired shots at them with a pistol that had been issued to him a month earlier, for personal protection. Liam was hit in the head and back and died three days later in hospital. In January 1983, the 34-year-old UDR soldier was sentenced to life for murder. In the course of that trial he admitted to wounding another man hours before the attack on Liam Canning.

So, two of the boys peering innocently out of that 1975 photograph died violently in the Troubles. Another team member just escaped with his life after he survived a gun attack intended to kill him. That casualty rate would not be untypical of GAA clubs in the Belfast area during the worst years of the political violence. The most poignant thing is that it was usually the younger members of the teams who were targeted. The killings threatened to rip the heart out of many clubs and the amazing thing is that so many survived, and then thrived as the worst excesses of that time slowly faded into the background.

The effect of what happened on the surviving young boys from those scores of photographs throughout Northern Ireland

— those who have lived to see the beginnings of a peace settlement — can only be guessed at. They must have been damaged in one way or another by the violent deaths of young team-mates. That is something they will carry with them to this day and beyond. And the clear message which was being sent out by those deaths would not have escaped them either. In the Belfast of the 1970s and 1980s membership of the GAA was enough to set you apart and, to use the terrorist parlance, make you a legitimate target for violence and even death. Such was the antagonism towards and mistrust of the GAA that was allowed to prevail.

For years, this was never properly acknowledged. Of course, there were more malevolent and more potent forces at work in the society of the time but even that does not explain the repeated refusal to address the way in which the GAA members were being deliberately targeted. There weren't enough voices to stand up in protest and those who did stand up struggled to be heard. What ensued as a result of that inaction is both shocking and shameful in equal measure.

The other Devlin family members were just as much victims of this as was Gerry himself. But during the most difficult times they drew on the support of the wider GAA community in exactly the same way that Seán Fox's family had looked to them and others like them fourteen years before. Cards and messages of condolence streamed into the Devlin family home from GAA clubs all over Ireland, the US and Canada.

At the time, much of it passed by in a blur. But with some distance now separating him from those terrible days after Gerry's murder, Kevin Devlin is in a better position to assess the value and importance of that support. He is also looking to the future and ways of marking Gerry's life with a more permanent memorial.

> All those cards were important to have. It's like one big family, you know. And I've written a letter to all the members of the club suggesting that the ground now be named after Gerry. It's the members who are the club and it's them who do all the work behind the scenes.

Kevin Devlin is convinced that these are better times for the GAA. The killings and the bomb-attacks have stopped, and the St Enda's club can get on with the job of providing a cultural outlet for one of the fastest-growing areas in Belfast. GAA business has never been so good and the club boasts thriving under-age structures — a whole new generation of under-12s just like that photograph of sixteen years ago.

Of course, the antagonism towards the GAA still simmers on in some quarters — glass is still strewn on football pitches, goal posts are still cut down and arson attacks are attempted — but the situation has improved beyond recognition. The GAA in Belfast can now stand prouder than ever before; that in itself is a cause for optimism — guarded optimism, but optimism all the same. Kevin Devlin reflects:

> Definitely, when you compare it to the time not too long ago that the GAA and its members were named on the list of loyalist targets.... They said they were going to start then but to me they had been targeting the GAA for twenty years. The terrible thing is that we did lose people, members, who just didn't go up to the club during those times.

Kevin Devlin's commitment to the St Enda's club has never wavered, even after the death of his brother. The brothers were the first to go back up to the club after the pattern of sectarian murders looked like draining all the confidence out of the fretful and anxious membership. So it was after Gerry died, and Kevin remains as involved as he ever was — maybe more so. The club, he says, has been strengthened by what it has been through, and its innate survival instinct has been a real source of inspiration.

> The club gains a bit from those days, I think. Overall, we can only get bigger and stronger. Look at the set-backs we've had. We lost premises, built them again. We got our President shot and then we got our team manager shot outside the gates. I don't think there are too many GAA clubs that could have continued after all that, especially with the small number of members we have.

If the attacks and the murders have had an effect on St Enda's it has been at the older end of the spectrum. The age profile of today's membership is predominantly young; the threats and intimidation led to a haemorrhaging of members during the more difficult periods. In a deteriorating political situation it was hardly surprising that some became so concerned about their personal safety that the risk of being identified with St Enda's and the GAA was simply one that was too big to take. Many of them have never been replaced and that has had implications for the make-up of the club. According to Kevin:

> This club is second to none with regard to showing its character and coming back. But the problem I see is that we don't have as many of the older guys any more — the 60- and 70-year-olds — to guide the younger ones the way we were looked after during the early 1970s.

The cost, as ever, is a human one.

*

As the May Day sun begins to hide itself bit by bit behind the hills, the people of St Enda's are getting ready for the night to come. The Fox and Devlin families have been here all day, as integral a part of the modern life of St Enda's as Seán and Gerry were when they were alive.

The prosperity of the club and its bright future are good reasons for everyone to celebrate. But this has been an occasion for looking back as well, and there is no shame in that. The cost to both families of involvement with the GAA has been immense, and that nagging sensation of the loss of a father, a son or a brother is one that never really goes away.

Nonetheless, that is something the Foxes and Devlins have to come to terms with. That is what Kevin Devlin is doing, and when he remembers, he remembers with fondness and tenderness. There is no bitterness.

> Any acknowledgement of Gerard, especially when it's related to the GAA, is very welcome for the whole family. My mother's still living and she's a great GAA woman because when my father was alive she had no choice really. There were just two or three sets of jerseys to be washed and then all our gear as well and that was it.

The pain, though, never recedes completely.

> As you can imagine, the GAA was a big part of our lives, so any recognition would definitely make my mother very proud. It must have been very hard for her. I lost my best friend and brother. But I think it's even worse to lose a son in circumstances like that. It's very difficult for people.

The games are over now, the Seán Fox Memorial Shield has been presented, and almost everybody has gone back inside. The big day out for St Enda's is over for another year. Even the ice-cream man has packed up. But out on the pitch are a few young hopefuls, aged maybe six or seven. Carrying hurls almost the same size as themselves, they are pulling and pucking to each other. To and fro. To and fro. The next generation. They look like they could keep going for hours yet, or at least until they're told it's time to go home. Seán Fox and Gerry Devlin would approve.

Chapter Four: A Good Son

Remembrance of things past. John McAnespie and his daughter, Eilish McCabe, look at each other. Their eyes meet and they start to laugh just a little self-consciously. They have just been talking about the footballing abilities of their son and brother, Aidan. Love and loss are in every word. With a hint of a smile, John recalls:

> Well, he wasn't the star player. But he was always there. You didn't have to push him into anything. With Aidan it would have been harder to keep him out. It was just here for him, all the crack and all the rest of it. When he was younger I would ask him every Saturday morning who they were playing today. He would say 'Caledon' because that was the next parish. The following Saturday you would ask him again and he would say 'Caledon again'. So it was always the same really.

With the merest hint of a grin, Eilish adds:

> You could depend on him. He was actually training to referee the younger boys' matches and he had been working with them. The last couple of times, in fact, before Aidan was shot I remember there was a real slagging match in the pub and in our house because any time Aidan went out he got injured. He had a bad knee and the knee kept getting dislocated on him and giving him bother. There didn't need to be anyone near him for Aidan to get injured with this knee — it would just go out on him.

By now the fondness of the memories is filling the small front room of the McAnespie family home in the Tyrone village of Aughnacloy, perched on the edge of the border with Monaghan and the Republic. 'We are a junior club,' John McAnespie says. 'And Aidan played for the reserve team so....'

All the implications of the quality of the football played at that lowly level are left hanging in the air. The reserves. There may be little beauty in the football played there, but what it lacks in finesse it more than makes up for in commitment. This is the GAA coalface.

A father and a daughter catch each other's eye and allow themselves another half-laugh, filled with love and longing. After a few seconds they both look away; the laughter ebbs away into the corners of the room and then it stops. It is replaced by a heavy, sad silence.

*

21 February 1988. Spring was doing its best to shake off the shackles of winter. It was a beautiful, frosty, sunny morning in Aughnacloy. It had been a busy weekend for the McAnespie family and, as usual, Aidan was at the heart of it. An aunt — his mother's sister — had died just a mile on the other side of the Tyrone–Monaghan border. On Friday Aidan and his mother travelled together to attend the wake. These journeys over and back across the border had taken a familiar pattern by now. Aidan had been working in Monaghan but found himself stopped repeatedly at the joint army and RUC checkpoint when he was going to and coming from work.

Eventually he decided to circumvent all the delays by leaving his car on the Monaghan side of the border. Every morning he would walk the short distance from the house to the border and go across on foot, pick up the car and drive on to work. And every morning his mother would go with him and see him safely through the checkpoint.

In the evenings, Aidan would drive back to the usual spot, lock up his car and walk through again to Aughnacloy. There to meet him every day would be his mother who had cycled down. It was not typical behaviour or a normal routine for a young man in his twenties and his mother. But then these were not normal times.

All through Friday, Mrs McAnespie and her son stayed together at the wake house in Monaghan and looked after the mourners who had called to pay their respects. Day turned to night and they sat up together with the body in the traditional country way. The next morning they came home. They had decided to take the car across because it would be needed for the funeral the following day. John McAnespie remembers:

> It was lovely weather at the time — dry, but a cold frosty morning. So they were coming back across the border and when they were going through the checkpoint they were stopped in the car by a soldier. They were driven down to the shed. They searched the car and it was the same thing with all the bad manners as usual. They told the wife she was just there to protect her son.

On the accepted scale of things, there was nothing out of the ordinary in any of this. Confrontation, threat and tension were part of the vernacular of this border area, and neither Aidan nor his mother had any reason to see anything particularly sinister in the way they were being treated on this Saturday morning. The people of Aughnacloy had grown used to the tension that permeated life there. But twenty-four hours later, Aidan McAnespie would be dead.

His aunt's funeral was on Sunday morning. Afterwards, Aidan came back to Aughnacloy. It was an important day, full of optimism and expectation, because it marked the start of the new football season. Aidan's club was Aghaloo and this was the team's first big chance to kick things off in style — a Tyrone county league game against Killeshil. Aidan was injured — that troublesome knee again. He'd started to wonder if it would ever be right. Would he ever get back to the reserves?

Still, he would be at the match all the same. He couldn't miss the first day of the year, that time when, for the first hour of the season at least, everything seems possible: not a single tackle missed; every free kick nonchalantly converted; one point after another; goal after goal. Championship. Promotion. Who knows?

4: A Good Son   43

The uncertainty of it all and the weight of heady expectation are all part of the appeal.

Aidan couldn't miss being part of the rhythm of the GAA life-force, taking his place for another year in the midst of his GAA tribe. Even though he wasn't playing he would go along to support his club. Besides, there was a good chance of some crack because he had been to school with some of the Killeshil boys.

But before that, there was work to be done — all the little jobs around the house that were part of his daily routine. He lit the fire out in the kitchen so that the house would be warm for his mother and father coming back from the funeral. Then he had to go out the back and feed his calves. He had bought two just as a bit of a hobby; maybe, if he was lucky, he might make a bit of extra money out of them. It all helped.

When he came back inside, it was football time. Aghaloo's ground was a short walk beyond the far side of the checkpoint. To save some time and hassle, Aidan decided to drive down as far as the border crossing and walk the rest of the way — he had become used to finding ways to avoid confrontations.

The events of the rest of the day are indelibly mapped out in John McAnespie's memory.

> After he fed the calves he headed down to the football match. They were playing Killeshil and he was looking forward to it because he would have known a lot of the Killeshil ones from going to school with a lot of them. He left his car on this side of the checkpoint at a place called Coronation Park and walked through. And he got a few hundred yards out the road when he was shot just before he got to the field.

At Coronation Park, at around ten to three, Aidan had met two other men — Paddy Mullan and his father-in-law. They too were leaving their cars on the northern side of the checkpoint before going across to the game. The three set off together down the hill towards the border crossing. Paddy, though, had forgotten something in his car and said he would go back to get it. His father-in-law went with him, so Aidan walked on alone.

By the time Aidan had reached the other side, he could just see the Aghaloo ground down below the road. It was a few minutes before throw-in and they were getting ready for the game. As Aidan McAnespie walked on, with his back to the checkpoint, three bullets were fired from a machine-gun in the British Army sangar behind him. One of the bullets killed him instantly.

John and the rest of the family were on their way home after the funeral.

> Paul was with me in the car and he said: 'There's Seán Mullan behind us — he wants us to stop.' So Paul, he got out of the car and went back. Seán told him Aidan was shot. I suppose at best you thought to yourself that he was just injured or something. But the blood just stopped in your veins.

Down at the checkpoint, players, officials and spectators from both teams had heard the gunfire and were by now gathered around Aidan McAnespie's body. Eilish McCabe remembers:

> We didn't know what had happened so we went down to see. When we got there all the footballers were there, all the Killeshil players and all Aidan's friends were around the body.

Eilish and the rest of the McAnespie family have spent the thirteen years since Aidan's death trying to piece together the truth about what happened at the checkpoint, and everything that followed immediately afterwards. Aidan's car, which had been parked at Coronation Park, was moved after the shooting, but the only set of keys to the car was found on Aidan's body. The family reported it stolen and it was only then that the RUC revealed that they had taken it to Dungannon. There are many more questions than answers. Eilish McCabe says:

> Less than an hour later the story being put out was that it was an accident. But how could they have known it was an accident without ever having questioned the person responsible? The whole checkpoint was closed. Dad and I went to the morgue in the ambulance with Aidan's body. Paul drove behind us and there were police cars behind that again.

By the time they got back to the family home at around eight o'clock that evening, local people had already started to arrive. The news of what had happened had travelled fast. 'It never stopped but you were in a kind of a trance as well, you know, not really aware of what was going on.'

The next day, Monday, followed the same pattern until somebody told the McAnespies that traffic was again being prevented from going through the checkpoint and that they had heard shooting. The McAnespie family believe they know why. 'When we got the news that the road was closed,' John says, 'Eilish just turned to me and said: "Daddy, they're marking the road."'

His daughter believes that this is the only possible explanation.

> There was a red light at the spot where Aidan was shot. We know that the only reason the road was closed was so that those three shots could be fired to support a theory that the bullet had ricocheted off the road.

*

Aidan McAnespie was not the first member of the Aghaloo club to die in violence during the Troubles. Because of its strategic position on the border, Aughnacloy had traditionally been a garrison town. The presence of the British Army in the village prompted obvious tensions. The fortifications and a generally strong security presence had long been a way of life in the village.

Mutual mistrust between the Protestant and Catholic communities which lived cheek by jowl in this small place was also a constant part of daily life. By the early 1970s, the GAA was already an obvious target for loyalist paramilitaries. Many were reluctant to become too closely involved in the workings of the Association; the fear had already set in.

Francie McCaughey had no such qualms. He was an active member of the GAA and an important figure in the Aghaloo club — just the kind of clubman Aidan McAnespie would be fifteen years later. Throughout 1973, the local farmer had been helping to put together a plan to buy some land for the Aghaloo club. The intention was to build the club's own pitch on it.

For Aghaloo, as for many clubs of its size, this was a significant aspiration, a sign that it could stand on its own two feet. Having your own ground meant independence and signalled ambition. Eventually a suitable field was found behind the RUC station, and the club at last had a home. Francie had played his part and the dream was about to become reality.

On the morning of 8 November 1973 Francie McCaughey went as usual to help with milking at a nearby farm. Some time later, his brother heard a loud explosion and arrived to find Francie seriously injured and dying. The door of the dairy had been booby-trapped. Responsibility for the killing was later claimed by a caller purporting to represent the Aughnacloy UFF. The murder was a body blow to the Aghaloo club. 'They still have that land Francie had been buying and it's never been touched,' says John McAnespie.

Membership of the GAA in Aughnacloy — as in countless towns, villages and townlands throughout Northern Ireland — set neighbours apart from one another. John McAnespie was a founder member of the Aghaloo club and still values its cultural importance.

> It was very important because it was a way of communicating with the rest of the county. Aidan would have known all the players throughout the county as well as those in his own area. I suppose only for the football and things like that, you wouldn't get to know people in the same way.

Despite that, during the Troubles the GAA did not operate in a rural idyll of goodwill and broad popular support. However non-political the intentions and motivation of those involved at grass-roots level, the Association still represented a potent badge of identity and belonging. This, in turn, spawned a *de facto* kind of segregation of mind-sets in the community that surrounded it. According to Eilish McCabe:

> With the Protestant community here, the GAA would be viewed as something alien. You have a lot of people who are in the security forces living in the town as well. The young people sensed that kind of thing where you felt that you were alien and that people were trying to alienate you in the community

because they didn't trust the GAA. There has always been mistrust here and fear among the GAA people in the town.

The rapid integration of violence into everyday life during the 1970s hardened attitudes and closed minds: them and us. The GAA continued to have a significance that went beyond the mere playing of football or hurling, and its influence was celebrated and demonised in equal measure by the opposing sides. In the main, though, it was allowed to go its own way in that peculiarly Northern brand of sporting apartheid.

The attitude of those on the outside looking in was one of general indifference; this was reflected in a refusal by the mainstream media to allocate the same air-time and column inches to Gaelic games as were given over to other local sports. The GAA community was not overly exercised. For many the sense of isolation was something from which they could even draw strength: themselves alone and all that. The situation was one of uneasy relative calm, and there is every indication that this would have persisted had it not been for other, outside influences.

These external forces arrived primarily in the heightening of security and the arrival of the British Army. The army established a permanent presence in Aughnacloy in the early 1970s, the most visible manifestation of which was the positioning of checkpoints both within the village and further out the road towards the border with the Republic. This had significant implications for the GAA club.

After Francie McCaughey's murder in 1973, plans to move to a new ground were shelved and Aghaloo continued to play its games at its field on the Monaghan Road on the outskirts of Aughnacloy. The problem was that players and spectators travelling to the field from the Aughnacloy side would have to pass through one and sometimes two army checkpoints. Antagonism towards the GAA quickly became an unavoidable part of the games themselves. John McAnespie says:

> That was a problem that was more or less there. There would have been a lot of players and individuals who suffered harassment from the army and the RUC. And then the very big

problem we had down there was the field. Whenever the army or the police or whoever would set up at the checkpoint on the Monaghan Road, that was a problem for a lot of people going through that and then on to the football.

Every facet of GAA life in Aughnacloy was affected, from the senior footballers and their hard-fought matches with rivals from the neighbouring parish, to the schoolgirls taking their first hesitant steps. The attentions of the security forces were a constant irritant, according to Eilish McCabe, and the inevitable by-product was resentment and anger. The constant attention and repeated confrontations made accommodation between both sides impossible.

> I remember us coming in and out to football matches, leaving from the house here, and there would be a lot of hassle going in and out of the checkpoint. Even when we were playing camogie, going out there with the camogie bags, they would be looking to search your bags and everything, even then.

The situation got so bad that even visiting teams would travel as far as the housing estate just beside the main checkpoint, leave their cars there, and walk through. That is exactly what Aidan McAnespie did on the day he was killed. It seemed a way of defusing the situation and meant that at least there could be some sort of guarantee that games would start on time. The alternative was one- and even two-hour delays inside the army complex as cars and kit-bags were searched and re-searched.

The McAnespie family members were wearily familiar with the routine.

> Our boys would all have played a bit of football but it would have been Seán who was the footballer in the house. He was the eldest and he would have been getting a lot of bad hassle going through the checkpoints. And if you had your football gear, you were sure to get stopped.

The McAnespies believe that the impetus for this attitude which was so prevalent among the young soldiers and RUC officers on the ground was passed down from their superiors and that there was a concerted effort within the security forces to single out GAA members for special attention. According to John:

> They hadn't a clue but I'm sure it was what they were told to do. It was like *One Man and His Dog* and those sheep trials. You can talk about the great dog that man had and all the rest of it but it was the man handling it that really did it all. They had their handlers as well.

By the 1980s, Aidan McAnespie had followed the well-trodden family path and was an enthusiastic member of the town's GAA club. In a place like Aughnacloy, there wasn't much to do for a young man of his age, and the club provided an important outlet. Aidan threw himself enthusiastically into everything. Even now his contribution is fondly remembered by his father: 'He was a good club man. If there were ever jobs needed to be done or that sort of thing, Aidan was there.'

Working across the border in a poultry factory in Monaghan, Aidan McAnespie was quickly picked out for special attention as he travelled to and from the factory every day. The family recalls one eleven-day period a year before he was shot, when they catalogued ten incidents of Aidan being stopped, searched and held for varying periods of time at checkpoints. On another occasion, his father was told by a soldier at a checkpoint that he had a bullet in his gun for Aidan. The message that was being sent out was chilling in its clarity. By the time of his death the situation was close to intolerable. Eilish McCabe says:

> It was pretty bad because there would be days Aidan would be coming home from work and he would be kept maybe two-and-a-half hours. There was a big shed you would have had to drive into and when they closed that door behind you it was pretty terrifying. There were times Aidan was scared himself.

On one rainy night he was stopped yet again.

> The soldiers asked him to take off his shoes and socks — it was bucketing out of the heavens at the time — and Aidan said 'No, I'm not, because it's raining.' And they jumped on him, pulled him to the ground and pulled his shoes and socks off on the side of the road. They searched him and after that he came up to our house. He was clearly very shook up and I said he would definitely need to report it. My husband was there and he said

he would go down to the police barracks with him and make an official complaint. You could see the marks around his neck where the soldiers had actually held him down and sat on his chest. He made the complaint and came back up home again.

The incident did not end there, however.

When Aidan was going to work the next morning a soldier waved at him when he went past through the checkpoint. When he got to Monaghan, Special Branch were waiting for him and arrested him. One of his friends in work called us to say he had been arrested. We went straight up to the Garda station — they had put him in a cell and never questioned him about anything. When we arrived they said: 'Oh aye, you can take him with you.' It was all part of the same system because they knew he had been on and that a complaint had been made the evening before.

On one occasion in 1986 Aidan McAnespie had been taken for questioning to Gough Barracks in nearby Armagh. He was never charged with any offence and after his death the RUC confirmed that he was not wanted for questioning in relation to any incident.

*

Aidan McAnespie's death in the early part of 1988 came at a tumultuous time. Just over a fortnight later, three IRA members were shot by the SAS in Gibraltar. Those deaths were followed by three more at the subsequent funerals in Belfast's Milltown cemetery, when loyalist Michael Stone launched a grenade and gun attack on mourners.

Just three days after that, two British Army corporals were killed at the funeral of one of Stone's victims in west Belfast. Even by the standards of the upside-down value system that operated at the time, this was a stark and terrifying period. There was a sense of death stalking itself as each funeral was itself marked by another killing. They were dark, nervous times.

Even in the midst of this savage cycle of recrimination, the shooting of Aidan McAnespie attained a particular prominence, a prominence which it has retained to this day. This was due, at least in part, to the circumstances, in particular the fact that he had been killed on his way to a Gaelic football match and within sight of the local GAA pitch. The Association was propelled to a position of prominence, and many within it, especially in the Republic, felt uneasy at the prospect.

For the first time since the hunger strikes of 1981 the GAA found itself pushed onto the political centre-stage and subjected to the harsh glare of media attention. The discomfort was obvious and was not eased as high-ranking officials found themselves facing questions. These questions centred mainly on the previous silence of the Association with regard to the campaign of security forces harassment which Aidan McAnespie and many young members of the GAA had been alleging for years. A GAA blind eye may have been turned to those allegations of harassment in the past, but the McAnespie shooting meant the time for equivocation was over.

Eilish McCabe was one of those looking for some answers.

> Everyone knew what was happening with the harassment. The GAA knew what was happening as well. They only got involved after it was too late really. The GAA in Tyrone were very aware of the difficulties with that checkpoint at Aughnacloy and the harassment that players from other clubs were getting as well.

However, to the dismay of the McAnespie family those issues had never been addressed.

> The GAA never stood up to it, to that checkpoint and the positioning of it. There were never any official GAA statements when young girls were getting bad harassment down there. I remember even after Aidan was shot there was a really bad incident with fellas coming back from a football match and they were scared to get out of the car. Aidan's case was the only time the GAA did publicly acknowledge that their members were getting harassed at vehicle checkpoints.

After the shooting of one of its members, the GAA hierarchy had little option but to take up a prominent position. The McAnespie family still talks appreciatively of the active role taken by the then President of the GAA, Mick Loftus. Together with officials from both the Tyrone county board and the Ulster Council, Mick Loftus attended Aidan's funeral — just as ten years later Joe McDonagh would go to the funerals of GAA members killed in the Omagh bombing.

The wider, grassroots GAA family also provided a framework of support. This willingness to stand alongside victims and their families is one of the recurring themes of the GAA response to events during the Troubles. It has never been forgotten. 'I suppose there were a lot of people from throughout the country who gave us an extra bit of support because of the GAA link,' says John McAnespie.

Eilish McCabe believes that the reaction of ordinary people also kept the pressure on an at-times-reluctant GAA to press for answers to the many questions thrown up by the killing.

> It definitely did because I think it was seen as a very definite attack on the GAA. There were cards coming in here from clubs all over Ireland, every corner of the country. I don't think there would have been an inquiry south of the border had Aidan not been a member of the largest sporting organisation in Ireland.

Whatever about reservations and concerns about the GAA being shoehorned into a more political role, Mick Loftus was forthright and direct in a number of statements he made after the McAnespie killing. At the GAA's annual Congress in Bundoran, just over a month later, he put harassment of members right at the top of the Association's agenda. His speech remains one of the most forceful and most influential contributions by any high-ranking official during the Troubles. It was one of the first signs that the GAA had decided that it could no longer stand dispassionately on the sidelines with regard to the situation in Northern Ireland. Mick Loftus said:

> It is incontrovertibly evident to any careful observer that members of our Association in those counties are being singled out and harried by the forces of law simply because they are GAA members. We cannot and do not make any unfounded claims about general blamelessness. And we protest that it is equally wrong for officers of the law to make judgments of entire blame. And we protest that it is unjust that suspicion is backed up by harassment.

The shooting of Aidan, he argued, was part of this wider process.

> I assure Congress that to my certain knowledge the death of one of our members on his way to a game in Aughnacloy is but the tip of the iceberg of continuing and deliberate harassment of our members.

Perhaps most interestingly, Loftus's comments did not end there. The President went even further and placed himself right at the centre of the political debate, with both a condemnation of the current violence and a reaffirmation of the GAA's core ideals.

> No thinking person, much less any native of Ireland, can be unmoved by the tragedies and outrages which are in many senses close to us. The GAA hopes and works for unity. It equally puts away and totally renounces any recourse to violence as a means to an end.

In contemporary media reports the outspoken comments of Mick Loftus were seen as being a direct reaction to the McAnespie shooting. In many ways they were, and the President tapped into the prevailing sense of both anger and helplessness among GAA rank-and-file members in Northern Ireland. However, over a decade on, and in the context of everything that has happened since, the death of Aidan McAnespie and the responses to it can be seen to have marked a watershed for the GAA.

Whether the Association liked it or not — and all the signs indicated significant unease — it was now a player in the wider political process in Northern Ireland. The shooting dead of one of its members by a British soldier could hardly have produced a different result. The GAA had no tenable option but to respond and involve itself in the debate that ensued. In the years that followed, this new political role became increasingly apparent as GAA officials regularly found themselves commenting on contemporary political issues. They may not always have been comfortable doing so but the practicalities of the situation now left them with little alternative.

However, for every action there is a reaction, and the impact on the GAA was that it became a much more visible target for loyalist paramilitaries who clearly regarded themselves as in some way empowered by the GAA's new prominence.

The forthright criticism of the security forces also had an impact. Rightly or wrongly, the GAA was regarded as being lined up in opposition to the RUC and the British Army. The inevitable response was to focus attention on Rule 21 of the GAA rule book, which prohibited members of those security forces from being members of the Association. In the years after 1988, Rule 21 was to become a live issue in the political and cultural life of the GAA. It is a debate which has rumbled on throughout the protracted peace processes and into the reform of the policing service.

The shooting of a local GAA activist at an isolated border checkpoint on the border between County Tyrone in Northern Ireland and County Monaghan in the Republic thus had a profound effect, and the aftershocks continue to be felt today. The GAA could never be the same after that late winter afternoon in February 1988. It had become an organisation with an unavoidable political dimension, and there was no turning back.

*

The bereaved members of the McAnespie family have watched with passionate interest the GAA's development throughout the years since Aidan's death. From the outset, the official investigation into what happened at the checkpoint on that February afternoon was surrounded by obfuscation, and the years since then have been spent trying to establish the truth. At times that search has been traumatic and deeply upsetting.

An 18-year-old Grenadier Guardsman, Jonathan Holden, was charged with unlawful killing, but he was never convicted. He claimed that he had been cleaning his weapon when his finger slipped, discharging three shots. One of these, he said, ricocheted and hit Aidan McAnespie. Holden was later discharged from the army. Right from the beginning, Eilish McCabe disputed his version of events and the ricochet theory.

> There was a girl and her mother coming up to the checkpoint directly under the line of fire and they heard one shot. They heard one shot. There were people in other cars as well and all they heard was one shot.

As Aidan was being buried, the family continued to raise doubts about the official version of what had happened. These doubts gradually became more concrete, and eventually the family made representations to the Irish government, demanding an independent inquiry. The government's response was to set up a Garda team, led by Deputy Commissioner Eugene Crowley. Given the clear lack of certainty as to the manner in which Aidan died, a dramatic course of action was taken.

Nine days after his death, Aidan McAnespie's body was exhumed and a second autopsy was carried out by the state pathologist in the Republic, John Harbison. The body was reburied some hours later. The family was distraught but intent on receiving answers. Eilish McCabe remembers:

> When the body was taken to Monaghan for the second autopsy it was discovered that part of the ribcage had been missing. We had never been notified that any part of the body had been removed for any reason.

In tandem with this, an independent ballistics expert was engaged by the McAnespies' legal representatives. The cumulative effect of both of these investigations was to cast considerable doubt on the official version of events. Every detail was challenged. Eilish McCabe continues:

> It wasn't even conclusive that the shot was actually from the checkpoint. He was shot through the chest and the bullet went out through the lower part of his back. And Aidan was facing the checkpoint when his body was found, even though he was actually walking towards the football field.

Eilish and the rest of the family have become convinced that Aidan's killing was not the accident it had been portrayed as.

> The independent ballistics expert carried out his own tests and he said that for a finger to accidentally slip on a trigger, it would take nine pounds of pressure to release that trigger. And the soldier made two conflicting statements. In the first he had said that he been cleaning a wall, that his finger was wet, and so when he touched the gun it had accidentally gone off. Then in another statement he said that he had been cleaning the sangar wall, that his hands were wet and he had lifted the gun out because he was cleaning it. He then said he passed it to another

soldier and it was then that his finger slipped on the trigger and it had gone off.

This conflict only created more doubt and more scepticism about the official version of the circumstances surrounding the shooting of Aidan McAnespie.

> Firstly, they wouldn't be cleaning a loaded weapon. Secondly, the weapon wouldn't have been cocked, and thirdly, the safety catch wouldn't be off. There are just so many inconsistencies.

The inherent connection between Aidan McAnespie's death and the GAA has ensured that the incident has retained a high public profile. The GAA dimension has been a useful tool in attracting media interest, and the family has used the publicity as a lever and a means of prompting official action. But the entire experience has been a chastening one for all of them. The journey towards the truth has proved long and tortuous. Eilish McCabe says:

> We know what happened but it's proving it. Aidan had made statements before that and had made complaints to the RUC directly but no member of the security forces has ever been disciplined. So it didn't come as a surprise to us that there was no one ever convicted of his murder either. There was a person initially charged and even the way he was treated in comparison to someone else who would be on the charge of unlawful killing — he got a couple of months in custody and when he was released, he was able to go on holidays with his family in England because they were having difficulties coming to visit. The DPP then announced that all charges against the soldier had been dropped because of insufficient evidence. We never expected anything else.

The official inquest into Aidan's death also proved to be a frustrating and ultimately futile exercise. There was controversy from the outset when the family sought to have the soldier involved attend and give oral testimony. He was instead permitted to make a written statement. The net result, according to Eilish McCabe, is that the family now have serious doubts about the nature of his involvement.

> We didn't see his statement, we never got access to it. He just made an unsworn statement for the inquest. All the papers you

see have said that Aidan was killed when on his way to play a Gaelic football match. But people close to Aidan knew that he wasn't playing because he had this knee injury from the last match he had played. And, as usual, when he wasn't playing he was going to watch.

Thus, the official version of the circumstances surrounding Aidan McAnespie's death, which has been in the public domain ever since the killing, may be fundamentally flawed. Aidan was not on his way to play in a football match and this key error casts doubt on everything else that has been said about the incident by those charged with investigating it.

> The soldier in his statement said he had observed Aidan parking his car in Coronation Park, taking his football bag out of the back of the car and walking through the checkpoint with his football bag. Aidan never had a thing in his hand — one arm was as long as the other — because he wasn't playing. But we've never had that person in a courtroom to challenge that statement; we've never been allowed access to him. That's what makes us convinced that it wasn't even him that did it.

Any confidence that the relatives might have had in the entire process melted away. They were being frustrated at every turn and it rapidly became clear to them that there were vested interests determined to ensure that they would not be allowed to ask uncomfortable questions and hold the relevant individuals to account.

The significance of the killing of Aidan McAnespie was that it had occurred as he was on his way to a GAA match; that context has had an important effect on the Association itself. Through Mick Loftus, the then President, the GAA became involved at an early stage in the days after Aidan's death, and that involvement continues to this day. This was not the first time that a member of the Association had been killed in the course of the Troubles. But it was unusual in that this was the shooting of a GAA member actually on his way to watch a game of Gaelic football. The linkage was there — inherent in all the circumstances of Aidan McAnespie's death — and the GAA has found itself politicised as a direct result. There was and is simply no escaping the connection.

The McAnespies deliberately concentrated their attentions on the government in the Republic. This, in itself, was an approach with a very clear political dimension — it sent out the message that they felt they could not expect satisfaction by pursuing the matter through British government channels in Northern Ireland. The GAA, by implication, was part of this and was therefore closely associated with those sentiments.

Eilish McCabe and her father are now pressing hard for a truth commission, similar to the South African one which sat at the end of the apartheid era. This, they believe, would be the only kind of forum that could get right to the truth, because it would be empowered to examine and question every detail of Aidan's death. Only then would they be satisfied that justice to Aidan's memory has been done.

> I think we will get to the truth. There is a soldier who went AWOL around the time of the shooting. I think he wanted to tell the truth but they told him not to bother coming forward at all. You might have to wait a while but the truth always comes out. It always does. And you can't move forward into some new process until the wounds of the past have been healed. That hatred that was there with the army has never gone. It's still there.

Until there is some form of resolution, the McAnespie family can only cling to the memories of the son and brother it lost. Eilish McCabe says:

> Despite everything that happened to him Aidan always remained very dignified. He never lost his cool and he never gave abuse back. He spoke very little and I think that he just got to them. He had become a thorn in their side.

The McAnespies had always been GAA people. John had been there right from the start with the Aghaloo club and that passion for the games and the Association was passed down to his children. Aidan, in turn, had taken his place within that tradition.

Before Aidan's death nobody in the family had been particularly aware of the wider GAA community. There was the club and the sense of belonging to that and playing a part within it. Beyond that, there was Tyrone and the passion around championship time for your county side. But there was never that feeling of real community — of a large, otherwise disparate collection of individuals, bound together by a shared identity and common values.

That sense became apparent only in the days and weeks after Aidan was killed. The support structures of the GAA kicked in — spurred on no doubt by the particular circumstances of Aidan's death. Messages of condolence poured in from clubs all over the country and even though some higher-ranking GAA officials may have been uncertain as to how they should respond, the grass roots were clearly not hidebound by the same political or strategic concerns.

The importance of all of this to the McAnespies was inestimable because it was an indication that they were not alone. There were considerable forces ranged up against them but there was never any feeling of total isolation. There were many GAA people from similar backgrounds, and with their own stories to tell, prepared to line up and support them.

That support could be found anywhere the GAA had established a presence. One of the greatest honours, and the thing the McAnespie family takes perhaps the most pride in, came with the setting up a of a new club in Boston on the east coast of the United States. The founding members approached the project with the same zeal as John McAnespie and the people of Aughnacloy had done a generation before. And when it came to naming that club they approached the McAnespie family and asked if they could name it after Aidan. The family was humbled by the gesture and gave its full approval. As they sat around and talked, the irony of a club being named after Aidan was not lost on them — the man from the Aghaloo reserve team was an unlikely figurehead. Eilish says:

> It was great honour for us, and it meant so much to think that these fellas who had never met Aidan wanted to name their new club after him. Aidan would have found it very funny as well because, you know, he wasn't the greatest footballer in the world. But here was a football team named after him. After they were formed, we went out to the annual dinner and were so well treated by all the people out there.

Aidan McAnespie's name would now always be kept alive and become part of the very fabric of the GAA. But this sad story was to twist cruelly one more time.

*

Fergal McCusker was from Maghera, County Derry. He was known to everyone as Rick. In 1997 he left Ireland to look for work in Boston. His brother was in the US as well, and he quickly found work in the building trade. Rick McCusker had time on his hands when he wasn't working and, like scores of emigrants to America before him, he gravitated towards the GAA. He had been an active member of the Watty Graham's club in Maghera before leaving Ireland.

The feeling of being part of Irish culture even though home was thousands of miles away made the transition a little easier. So Rick joined his local club — the one that had been named after Aidan McAnespie. Soon he was playing football with the team and had got himself a girlfriend from Boston. Life was good.

Towards the end of 1997, Rick came home to Maghera for a break. He intended to return to Boston in the spring. The building work would have picked up by then and he could get back to the football as well. He had got a job at home in the meantime. His girlfriend, who had never been to Ireland, stayed at home in the States.

Early on the Sunday morning of 18 January 1998 Rick was in the centre of Maghera. He had been out for the night with friends and was on his way home. At some point on that journey he was abducted by gunmen from the Loyalist Volunteer Force. Eyewitnesses reported that they had seen two men with their faces painted orange in the area at the time of the killing. The gunmen took Rick McCusker behind a local youth club and shot him at close range. His body was not found until the following morning.

The McCusker and McAnespie families now naturally established contact with each other; the connections between both deaths affected both families deeply. They now had the same terrible sense of loss in common. Rick McCusker's GAA background was celebrated at his funeral in Maghera and much of the old pain was reopened for the McAnespies. Eilish McCabe remembers:

> It was very hard for us at that funeral because as well as the shirt of his local club, the red and white shirt from the Aidan McAnespie club in Boston was also on the coffin.

The families stayed in touch and the McAnespies kept a keen eye on the football club in Boston. Later in 1998, Eilish and the rest of the family took part in some important celebrations.

> The club got to the All-American finals in San Francisco and they actually won it. We went out for the annual dinner again and it was Rick's brother who had been the captain of the team. When he went up to get the trophy, that was very emotional as well.

The wheel had come full circle.

*

The killing of Rick McCusker represents a full stop of sorts to the story of the life and death of Aidan McAnespie. The family's collective hunger for the truth remains as unfulfilled as ever, but the shared suffering with another GAA family is something from which they can draw strength.

The McAnespies can also take some comfort from the fact that the GAA was never quite the same after Aidan's death. The antagonism, harassment and physical abuse directed towards GAA members in Northern Ireland could never again be casually explained away by the security forces responsible.

The shooting dead of one of its own members by a British soldier forced the powers that be within the GAA to confront some difficult truths about the political and cultural life of Northern Ireland. Men and women were being repeatedly singled out for adverse treatment simply because of their GAA membership. After Aidan McAnespie's death, the GAA had to address this head-on. There could be no more running away.

Chapter Five: What Might Have Been

Promotion: Seán McNulty and the other members of the Warrenpoint senior football team could smell it in the air at the end of the 1981–82 season. In every county which professes even a passing interest in Gaelic football, getting into and staying in Division One of your league is all that really matters.

Everything else is nowhere. And in Down, a county with a patrician view of its own importance in Gaelic football's great scheme of things after its imperious All-Ireland successes of the 1960s, the lure of Division One was even more pronounced. It meant respectability and it represented achievement.

So it came to pass that on a Sunday afternoon at the tail-end of the 1982 season the Warrenpoint men had promotion within their grasp. The winter and early spring had gone well, better than they might have expected. Seán McNulty, an All-Ireland minor winner with Down five years before, was a central figure in this final, desperate push.

Helping his club to get back into Down football's top flight was the high point of his Gaelic football career up to that point. It was a defining moment. Seán McNulty was 21.

> My last game for Warrenpoint was in Newry. It was the last game of the season and we needed to win to get the promotion and back into Division One again. And we did, we won promotion that day.

During the days that followed, the town was engulfed in celebrations. When the glow of victory started to recede just a little, the minds of the real football people began to turn towards the new season and Division One. Already plans were being laid and strategies plotted to ensure that the club could hold on to what it had struggled so hard to attain.

However, Seán McNulty was by now a peripheral figure. He had already begun to put a distance between himself and everything around him. In his mind he was getting ready to leave, and deep down he knew that part of him had already left.

The rest of his Warrenpoint team-mates would be in Division One next year but they would have to face into it all without him. There was no other way, no viable alternative. Just one week after Warrenpoint made that short but triumphant journey home from Newry, Seán McNulty left his club and his home town for good. He has been back only occasionally and has never played football for Warrenpoint again. From that day forward, everything changed; there was no going back. Seán McNulty joined the Royal Ulster Constabulary.

*

For a schoolboy growing up in Down, the 1960s were a magical time. The decade was book-ended by back-to-back All-Ireland titles in 1960 and 1961, and then a third title in 1968. The legend of Down football had begun to grow, and aspiring young players like Seán McNulty could not help being carried along in the current.

> In Warrenpoint there was a very strong tradition of the GAA for me from an early age. In fact, I remember playing Gaelic football — I was probably about seven or eight — in the local primary school.

He remembers that from his earliest days there was an ecumenism at work in the town regarding its cultural life; this was to shape Seán McNulty's later life. Down has traditionally been a county which does things just a little differently from its Ulster neighbours.

The headmaster at that time was Ted Bradley and I'm sure he must have been one of the first ever headmasters in Northern Ireland to arrange a challenge match between the local Catholic and Protestant primary schools.

Just a few years later, an initiative like this would have been all but impossible. But this was the late 1960s and the tribal lines of division tended to be more glossed over and obscured than they would be just a few years later. The entire experience left its mark on the young Seán McNulty.

> I think the challenge was laid down that we played a soccer match between the two schools first — which we won — and the Gaelic match was the follow-up and we won that as well. But it was a one-off and I suppose at the end of the day it was just prior to the start of the Troubles in 1968–69. It's just a pity it wasn't followed up and exploited more.

Those primary-school experiences flowed seamlessly into secondary school and St Colman's College in Newry. The college had a proud record as a nursery for Gaelic football talent on both sides of the county border between Down and Armagh; in fact, that tradition continues to this day and the college has a shaping influence on the composition of the teams that represent both of those counties. Seán McNulty was a boarder for his first two years at St Colman's, and thrived in the football hothouse, moving through the ranks of Ulster colleges football from Corn na nÓg to Rannafast and then on to the holy grail of the school's MacRory Cup team.

Gaelic football had become part of the fabric of Seán's life, and his commitment to the ethic of the team overrode any cultural or political connotations that others would try to attach to his immersion in the world of the GAA.

> For me it was not really a cultural thing. It was more the dedication to the football itself and certainly when I was playing — especially for your club team — it was just an honour for the club team. Likewise for the college teams, to wear your college colours. You felt very proud.

By this time Seán McNulty was starting to attract the attention of some of the football *cognoscenti* within Down. He was young — still just 16 — but a place on the county minor team seemed like the next step. A natural reticence and some lingering doubts, however, played on his mind.

> I certainly didn't walk on to the team. In fact, I was a bit apprehensive about even going for the trials. I thought it was a bit out of my reach but I got the right sort of encouragement, from Seán O'Neill in particular.

The influence of Seán O'Neill — a totem and a touchstone on the great Down sides of the 1960s — fills the landscape of modern Down football, and even now, more than twenty years later, Seán McNulty talks about him with an air of reverence:

> I was the youngest on the team, just turned 17 when we played the All-Ireland final. But he pushed me to go for it and put me in the right frame of mind — positive thinking, dedication and training. His attitude was that you can do anything if you stick with it.

The templates that were set down with that minor team of 1977 were to serve the county well over the next twenty years. There was a particular emphasis on preparation and the fostering of team spirit — qualities that were to set apart the senior team of the early 1990s. Seán McNulty is proud to have been part of it.

> You were getting a lot of encouragement all the time. Come 1977 and that minor team you had the selection panel there — Seán O'Neill, Tony Hadden, Seán Lavery, Seán McManus — and it was just eat, sleep and talk football. They put an awful lot of effort into that team and I think that's the reason we were so successful.

There was also that special, indefinable sense of being part of something special, a one-off.

> There was great comradeship and camaraderie among the team. When you have players like John Toner, Ned Toner from Castlewellan, big Pat Donnan who was the Down goalkeeper for many years after that, Adrian McCaulfield, Paddy O'Rourke, who was the Down captain and lifted the Sam Maguire in Croke Park.

This team of all the talents ambled through the early part of the season, easily taking the Ulster minor league and then the minor provincial championship. The first day in Croke Park saw the challenge of Mayo calmly brushed aside and, on 25 September, Seán McNulty and the rest of the Down team faced Meath in the All-Ireland minor final of 1977. The stage was set.

> I can remember being very nervous going down on the coach. We stopped for lunch and again we were encouraged to think positive and focus on the game and concentrate. Again Seán O'Neill and Tony Hadden were involved in all of that. To be honest, the game itself went through from start to finish and I couldn't remember two or three minutes of the whole game. It's just a daze now. But the feeling at the end was unbelievable, all the excitement. It really is hard to explain because you're almost out of it.

Down won easily, scoring 2–6 in the process and conceding only four points. But this was a win that was about much more than just an early autumn afternoon in Croke Park. An All-Ireland title was a badge that could be worn for the rest of their lives by those who had helped win it, and it represented their entry into the great shared football folk history of Down football. Seán McNulty had become part of the proud tradition and that was something which could never be taken away from him. No matter what happened in the future.

Seán McNulty re-emerged the following year, with an All-Ireland medal tucked in his back pocket but still eligible for the minor grade. The lustre of the previous year — that sense of a journey into the unknown — had gone, however, and Down exited the Ulster minor championship in Casement Park at the hands of Tyrone. The memories of 1977 still glow brightly however, and, in fact, have become even more focused for Seán McNulty as a result of the direction his life has taken since then.

> It was a dream come true, certainly as far as my sporting career was concerned. And when I look back it's been the highlight of my career since as well. People always say: 'Oh, you're Seán McNulty, you're the boy who has the All-Ireland medal'. People know me as a footballer and I don't know who they are, no matter where I go.

How does that make him feel?

> Great, no problems at all.

5: What Might Have Been

*

In the years since, Seán McNulty has had ample opportunity to ponder the motivation that underpinned his decision to leave behind everything he had known in his life and join the Royal Ulster Constabulary. Even now, Catholics make up less than 10 per cent of the policing force, but back in 1982 when the Troubles were at their height, the recruitment of Catholics into the RUC had slowed to a barely quantifiable trickle. Seán McNulty could not have made a career choice more out of tune with the nationalist community into which he had been born and had lived for the previous twenty years.

However, as with his life-long affinity with the GAA, the ties had been forged, and the desire to be part of the police force had been there for as long as he could remember.

> The seeds had been sown from a very early age because we lived next door to a policeman and his wife would have looked after us when we were kids. I'm talking about from a very early age — five or six. But it wasn't a thing that you discussed openly around Warrenpoint, that you were going to join the police. Especially coming from a very nationalist background and being heavily involved in Gaelic football.

The reasons against joining were stacked up heavily against him. Primarily, there were the security considerations. In 1982, the year Seán became a policeman, 112 people were killed in Northern Ireland, among them twelve RUC officers. Personal safety became a monotonous feature of the regimentation of daily life; there was a persistent fear of attack. Joining the RUC meant becoming part of a grouping under continuous siege.

Beyond that, there was the extent to which a man from Seán McNulty's background made himself a social pariah in his own community by joining the police force. In the small town of Warrenpoint the decision by the All-Ireland medal winner soon became public knowledge.

> Oh yeah. When you left home to join the police it wasn't something that could be kept quiet. Everybody knew within a month. You just disappeared and people got talking when you

weren't down the pub for a pint on a Friday or Saturday night. In a small community like Warrenpoint, it didn't take long for word to get about.

None of this came as a major surprise. By the early 1980s, the Troubles had been around long enough for their patterns to have become embedded in Northern Ireland society. The framework of social and cultural rules may have been unspoken, but the far-reaching effect of those rules was well known. And all the implications of RUC membership, particularly for a nationalist or a Catholic, would have been glaringly obvious.

Seán McNulty, therefore, knew what he was getting himself into. He was less well prepared for the ripples and the aftershocks. The lines of division between the GAA and the security forces had long been drawn in Northern Ireland, and they found formal expression in Rule 21 of the GAA rulebook, with its explicit prohibition on members of the British security forces, including the RUC, from being members of the Association.

Throughout the middle part of the last century it was a rule more breached than observed, and an administrative blind eye was turned to any transgressions. The renewal of violence in Northern Ireland in 1968 changed all that. It quickly became apparent that, in addition to the street protests, the bombings and the gun attacks, there was a cultural and social struggle running in parallel. The re-emergence of the IRA and the arrival of the British Army were physical manifestations of a battle for superiority that was being fought between Irishness and Britishness. Within that contest, guns, explosives and petrol bombs were replaced as weapons by flags, symbols and emblems. The marking out of territory with Tricolours or Union Jacks, the painting of kerbstones, the parading of cultural icons — they all quickly became part of the process.

In theory, the GAA, as an exclusively cultural and sporting organisation, operated outside or above all of this. The Association clung — desperately at times — to its avowedly non-political ethos and tended to use it as a shield to protect itself from any political fall-out. Laudable as this may have been, it gradually became a position that was both untenable and unsustainable.

In such an atmosphere Rule 21 was an inevitable battleground. For decades a blind eye had been turned throughout Northern Ireland to men with security forces — primarily RUC — connections continuing to be a part of the GAA. The stakes were not particularly high and there was no strong inclination to interfere with the status quo. The renewal of violence changed all that, and in the significantly heightened atmosphere those RUC men who had played football or hurling without so much as a second thought quickly became much more conscious of the security risks that they were now running.

For most, the issue was decided for them by the security risks, and they fell away from the day-to-day workings of the GAA; it was a peculiarly Northern Irish example of cultural wastage. That process of voluntary retirement meant that the GAA was not faced with any awkward situations of enforced suspensions or other punitive sanctions; an uneasy status quo prevailed. The GAA did not want any policemen or soldiers within its ranks and members of the security forces had no desire to put themselves at risk by being part of it.

None of this would have been any great surprise to Seán McNulty. Political and cultural tensions were a fact of daily life at the time and would have been very familiar to him. And yet he was totally unprepared for the most obvious and pertinent consequence of his decision to join the RUC — his playing career within the GAA was over. Although the GAA played a huge part in his life, he says that it was not something he weighed up before making up his mind.

> No, it wasn't actually. It was out of my mind completely that I'm going to miss the football. I think I got lost somewhere along the way and I became very disillusioned with the sport. I wouldn't say I regretted it immediately but certainly within the first year or two of joining the police it dawned on me that I had left the sport that had brought me so much success. When I did eventually join the police I just wasn't prepared for the vacuum it left. I got a lot of support from my family which helped me through it.

The situation was not helped by the fact that Seán McNulty was training three or four nights a week and on the verge of breaking into the Down senior football set-up. In the space of a few days he went from that level of intense commitment to nothing. The emotional come-down was very difficult to cope with, and there were times when the feelings of isolation spilled over into bitterness.

> There was a lot of resentment towards the rule but I can see why it was introduced. At the end of the day, for fellas like me who joined the police, I don't think anybody would have been stupid enough or naïve enough to say 'I'm going to keep turning out for my club team'.

The old pull was still there but it was now accompanied by a highly developed sense of pragmatism.

> Every Sunday you would have been putting the lives of your family on the line for a game of football. It was a very difficult time in 1982 — it was just after the hunger strikes and there was a lot of tension throughout Northern Ireland at that time. Really, it would have been total madness to think that you could join the police and turn out and play Gaelic for the club.

*

People who experience a sudden break in a fixed routine often experience great difficulties in the period after the routine has been broken. An extreme example is that of a hostage. The routine of the average hostage day becomes like a comfort blanket and source of protection. But when the hostage situation is ended, the status quo is shattered and that 'comfort' is taken away. In its place there is only a void.

In the months and years after he left behind his GAA routine to join the RUC, Seán McNulty learned all about this displacement theory. Cultural reference points were few and far between for a young Catholic growing up in Northern Ireland throughout the 1970s and the 1980s, and for many the GAA was a vital presence. The pattern of organised under-age games and the steady progression through the ranks of club — and, for the fortunate few, county — represented a framework on which everything else could be hung.

When Seán McNulty collapsed that framework around himself he found it difficult to shore up the gaping holes that had been left. Inevitably, he turned to sport but it was not sport as he had known it throughout his life.

> I started doing a lot of running and jogging and was playing a lot of soccer for the various police divisional teams. I started some training and ran a couple of half marathons and then the Dublin Marathon. That took quite a bit of training and dedication but once I had set my mind on it, there was nothing going to put me off.

For a while he achieved a certain level of contentment, and he even began to enjoy the new directions he was taking. But the memories of the GAA world he had left behind remained stubbornly just below the surface.

> I enjoyed it, but when I look at it now it was really just a substitute for the Gaelic, a way of filling the vacuum. It didn't fill it totally but it passed the time and certainly kept me in a high level of fitness.

He did try to keep up to date with Warrenpoint's progress back at home but the gap was already unbridgeable. Despite living less than an hour away, Seán McNulty would not and could not go back. The prospect of his going to see the club play on a regular basis receded with every passing day.

> I would have gone to the very odd one, but maybe only three or four games over the last ten years. I would be able to follow the club team by reading the reports in the paper. They were relegated and now they're back up again....

The sentence tails off because what remains unsaid is the hardest part of all to come to terms with — it all happened without him.

*

Catholics comprised less than 10 per cent of the RUC when Seán McNulty joined; a degree of isolation was thus part of the territory of the job from an early stage. His decision had already made him a stranger among many of his own people, and now he found himself part of a fairly insubstantial minority within his new working environment and world. A background in the GAA was another cultural marker of difference, and the attitudes of some of those around him surprised him in the early stages.

Around Championship time there was always a level of interest, and on a slow Sunday in the barracks it was not uncommon for the television to be switched on.

> Certainly when you got to the televised stages of the Championship a lot of fellas would sit down and watch it. They would look at some of the tackles and be amazed that guys could walk away from it. They talk about fitness levels for various sports but these guys could see that it must be one of the fittest sports going. There was definitely a lot of admiration from people you wouldn't have expected it of.

However, such reactions proved to be the exception rather than the rule. Among his own colleagues Seán McNulty also found an antipathy towards the GAA.

> There were one or two who would come in and, seeing the Gaelic football on in the station, would say: 'Who's watching that? Turn that off.' There was always one or two like that but that's their problem. It comes from a very narrow viewpoint. There weren't too many but you get the odd one.

It is no surprise that the prejudices against the GAA that run through Northern Irish society should be replicated amongst the personnel of the RUC. The connection made between the Association, nationalism and militant republicanism was a by-product of the cultural struggle that ran parallel to the physical violence during the thirty years of the Troubles. For all the ideology of a neutral police force, it was unrealistic to expect that the same mind-sets would not operate within the RUC. Nevertheless, Seán McNulty did not walk away. He fought his corner both for himself and for the GAA.

> The odd time there would have been a comment passed about the GAA being closely connected with the Republican movement. I took great exception to that because nothing could be farther from the truth. Gaelic clubs are there to promote Irish tradition and Irish sport and that's all it was. It was absolutely

nothing to do with politics or the armed struggle but some people were very hard to convince.

Perception was everything with regard to the public face of the RUC at this time, and the widely held belief was that GAA members and those associated in a broader sense with the games were singled out for particular attention by the police and the British Army.

The sequestration of land at Crossmaglen, and the systematic campaign of harassment documented by Aidan McAnespie in the months before he was shot have already been discussed. At the grass-roots level, the day-to-day attentions of the RUC during this period set GAA people apart from the rest of the population. On Sunday afternoons, checkpoints would suddenly spring up on the road to the local GAA pitch. Exhaustive Border searches would coincide with the exodus of GAA fans to Dublin on the Sunday mornings before important All-Ireland occasions at Croke Park. The message was clear. To be associated with the GAA was to set yourself apart.

Seán McNulty would have had a better awareness than most of the type of disruption such RUC attention could cause. Was he aware, then, of a deliberate campaign of harassment?

> I don't know if they were being deliberately targeted or not but I thought it was a very stupid policy where security forces were coming into contact with GAA members going to football and what have you. It created an unnecessary atmosphere and tension that you didn't need to introduce. It certainly did nothing to enhance the relationship between the police, the security forces and the members of the GAA clubs. And I think the gap widened then as a result of some actions of the security forces.

With significant numbers both of RUC members and of members of the general public predisposed against the GAA and what it stood for culturally, all it took was an incident or two to provide grist to their mill. Some of the publicity the GAA attracted during the Troubles was decidedly unwelcome and Seán McNulty again found himself on the defensive.

> I can see why some of the things that were done were in fact done. One incident in particular comes to mind. The clubrooms

in Ardboe were used for an IRA arms hide. You then got people saying that they had an IRA arms dump in that GAA club so they must all be the same. You tend to paint everybody with the same brush, which was totally unfair. I took great exception to that. It was highlighted and publicised and really did very little to enhance the reputation of the GAA.

He would like to think that, in his own small way, he did something to change hearts and minds. In many instances, the men and women he was talking to were being asked — for perhaps the first time in their lives — to take on board a point of view other than their own in relation to the GAA and its influence. Seán McNulty proved to be a persuasive advocate.

> If you know what you're talking about you can talk your way through any argument. But a lot of people didn't know their facts. They just said things like: 'The GAA all support the Provos and they're all into Republicanism.' I had to say: 'Hold on a minute. I've never seen that in fifteen years of my life playing Gaelic football.' They'd go: 'Oh right. I didn't know that now.' After they thought about it, some of them would actually have regretted their comments in the first place.

In the big scheme of things it may have made little difference. But to Seán McNulty it was progress and that mattered.

He makes no attempt to hide the harsher realities of his life since he joined the RUC and the very real difficulties he faced in removing himself from the GAA and all the cultural life that goes on around it. Even in the black-and-white world of Northern Irish politics, with its emphasis on placing people in one camp or the other, the effect of Rule 21 on men like Seán McNulty was unequivocal. He was never in any doubt about that.

> Yeah, basically it sends out the signal that you can't be a serving member of the police and a member of the GAA. That is effectively what it is telling you. You can't be both. It has be one or the other.

The rule and its rigorous application left no room for manoeuvre, and that was something Seán McNulty had to come to terms with. But that resignation did not protect him from some very difficult times. It was his misfortune to be living through all of this at precisely the same time that Gaelic

5: What Might Have Been

football in Down entered into a second golden age of All-Ireland success. Every fresh triumph carried pangs of regret in its wake.

The first stirrings of that football renaissance had begun during the latter part of the 1980s resulting largely from the graduation on to the county senior team of many of the minors who had played alongside Seán McNulty at under-age level. Seán himself was in his late twenties and somewhere near what should have been his Gaelic football peak. But right through it all he could only stand at a distance and watch.

The 1991 campaign was the toughest. The team captain for the year was the centre half-back, Paddy O'Rourke, a team-mate from the 1977 All-Ireland winning team. It was impossible not to make the connection and, just for a few seconds, wonder about what might have been. Seán followed Down's progress through the Ulster Championship and even managed to make it to the Ulster final against Donegal.

That game, like all Ulster finals, was played in the County Monaghan town of Clones, and so Seán McNulty's day out necessitated a trip across the border between Northern Ireland and the Republic. He made the journey with the minimum of fuss but afterwards there were some RUC colleagues who were a little more exercised by it.

> There'd be guys who would ask you: 'Were you at the game on Sunday in Clones?' When you said that you were they'd say: 'You didn't go to Clones did you, across the Border?' 'Aye, why not?' 'I wouldn't have been going.' Then I'd say to them: 'Well, nobody asked you to go.'

However, as Down marched inexorably on and it became clear that the team was not going to be content with an Ulster title, it became much harder for Seán McNulty to get to the matches. The cruellest cut of all came with the final itself against Meath. There was so much bound up in the occasion for him, particularly as it seemed to crystallise so many of the life decisions that he had made. But the party went on without him.

> That 1991 final was a very emotional occasion for me. Paddy O'Rourke, of course, was the captain, and he had played with me in 1977. It was great to see him there but I had work

commitments and couldn't get the day off no matter how hard I tried. It was the one day in the year I looked off. But that was it.

He busied himself through that September afternoon and managed to finish his shift early. The sole aim then was to get to see some of the game.

> I got home and then went to a local pub to watch it. The crack was ninety. It was unbelievable and it was a long evening. It was a very Gaelic-orientated pub and everybody knew who I was and what I was. But it was like: 'Oh, come in, come in, they've just started.' Unfortunately the licensing laws at the time didn't permit Sunday drinking, but nobody was any the wiser.

That engagement with the game and the whole occasion, even at a distance, was important to Seán McNulty. It was about belonging and experiencing his own little part of that shared cultural event. By the time 1994 and Down's second All-Ireland title of the decade came along, there were no problems with shifts, and he was at both the All-Ireland semi-final and the final.

Again it was not beyond the bounds of possibility that at the age of 34 he could have been part of that team as well. If thoughts like these are demons that Seán McNulty has had to confront over the years, it is a process he has approached with a fair degree of equanimity. He has never minded the speculation of others and, deep down within himself, he probably feels that they just might have a valid point. There have been times when he has imagined himself right there in the middle of it all.

> I think when you've played in a big game you really appreciate the occasion more. And I had it thrown up to me a few times in 1991, with Paddy O'Rourke as captain and all of that, that I should have been out there playing that day. A couple of guys I was watching the match with and having a beer with were saying those things. All I could say was that they could be right. If I hadn't joined the police ... who knows?

Seán McNulty is not a man who deals in regret. Too many difficult paths have been chosen along the way for that to be part of his life.

> I don't know if I would do it differently or not. I would have liked the ban to have gone before I joined the police but I just

think I was destined to be a police officer from a very young age, maybe six or seven years old. It was just difficult to come out and say something like that, and if it was made public you would have been intimidated to try and stop you making the move.

However, he does admit to a degree of wistfulness when he thinks that he could have been a contender.

I've definitely got mixed emotions and I have found myself thinking that if I'd stuck with the Gaelic career, if I had been training, looking after myself, dedicated, determined enough to keep at it, then I could have been on that team all right.

With their titles, the Down players had cut a swathe through thirty years of perceived wisdom about the inadequacies of Ulster counties when it came to the All-Ireland series. Neighbours and rivals were emboldened by the team's exploits, and All-Irelands for Donegal and Derry in 1992 and 1993 were examples of their ability to surf that wave of success.

By the time Tyrone took its place in the 1995 All-Ireland final Seán McNulty was stationed in the town of Coalisland in the eastern part of the county. Change was in the air on so many fronts and he had already begun to dip his toes tentatively into the GAA waters again. There was something that kept enticing him back.

I had served in Coalisland for six years. And there were Sunday afternoons when I'd be on duty and pull up and watch a match. It was the talk of the town for weeks, that Seán McNulty had pulled a police car into the grounds of the GAA club and watched a match. Quite a few people who I'd got to know in Coalisland through the GAA circles said: 'Did I see you at the match on Sunday?' I just said they had and that I had just called down to see how it was going.

It is a fantastic image — an unmarked RUC car parked in the grounds of the GAA club in a town like Coalisland, with its well-documented history of republican activity, and inside an All-Ireland medal winner straining out through the window to watch the game unfolding. Seán McNulty was also doing his own little bit of evangelising about the game.

Some of the people in the town had heard that I'd been explaining the rules to one of the officers who was with me, all about the difference between the ball going over and under the bar and that sort of thing. One them then said: 'Ah, you could be playing for us yet.' And that was always the sort of banter that went on between us: 'Ah, you could be playing for us yet....'

Seán's GAA credentials became a useful calling card in an area where antagonism towards the RUC as a whole would have been running high. It was something he used to his advantage, and it went some way to making what could have been a difficult, even threatening, situation just a little easier.

It certainly made you more acceptable, people knowing that you came from a Gaelic background. It broke down the barriers. Even doing these inspections of licensed premises at the GAA clubs. In the odd one or two you'd be offered a drink and if it was a Sunday evening the Championship highlights would have been on and you would watch them. I know there are very few police around Coalisland who would do that sort of thing. In fact I've never heard about it before or since.

In retrospect, it is clear that Seán McNulty was taking considerable risks; there were still on-going, serious threats to the personal safety of RUC officers from republicans. But he did it because it was a way for him to connect with something that he had left behind. The experience helped everything else make a little more sense.

I think people did see me as straight down the line — the McNulty who used to play football for Down. You could talk about football for an hour and then when you were leaving you'd ask yourself what you went in there for in the first place. In fact, on more than one occasion we had a drink or two and had to summon some help to get home again.

This relative informality to Seán McNulty's dealings with the people of Coalisland made the work he had to do a little easier. It was a community he felt part of in some small way, and so when it became consumed with All-Ireland fever in the summer of 1995 it was inevitable that he would get caught up in it too. His position of influence also had its advantages when it came to getting hold of tickets for Tyrone's final with Dublin but he is tight-lipped about his sources.

'Easy enough done,' he says. 'All it takes is a phone call. That's all.'

And so it came to pass that when Tyrone journeyed en masse to Dublin on that afternoon in late September 1995, Seán McNulty was there too.

> When Tyrone got to that final I was on Hill 16 amongst about 300 supporters from Coalisland, and not one of them ever saw me. Yet I could name at least twenty-five people who were standing within 10 yards of me. And the next day I was back on duty and I saw quite a few of them. With hangovers right enough.

*

None of this would have been possible without a dramatic relaxation in the security situation in Northern Ireland, and when Seán McNulty made his trip to the All-Ireland final in 1995 the IRA and loyalist ceasefires of the previous year were holding firm. It was around this time that he began to detect a change in the general mood.

> I think the GAA realised that it had to change with the political progress and the ceasefires coming into effect. The GAA had to review its attitude to Rule 21.

However, if a review was taking place, it was well away from the glare of publicity and resulted in very little movement over the next few years. While voices from Republic of Ireland members raised themselves intermittently to make their opposition to Rule 21 heard, it became almost an unspoken rule of the GAA that there would be no movement on the issue without the consent of the Ulster counties. The perception was that officials from those counties were best placed to judge the extent of any changes in the political landscape.

A motion sponsored by Sligo, Carlow, Down and Dublin did appear on the agenda for the GAA's Annual Congress in 1995, but it seemed to disappear into the ether without ever being debated on the floor. The internal discussions that surrounded the withdrawal of the motion were never made public but the thinly veiled explanation was that the Ulster counties — bar Down — were opposed, and without them on board no movement was possible. The irony that the lone Ulster voice against the rule came from his own county was not lost on Seán McNulty.

> I was actually surprised that it hadn't been done before but I think it is typical of the GAA clubs throughout Down that they wanted to see the ban lifted. It was great to see.

Nevertheless, the GAA remained against change. Looked at in any way, this seems an unusual position for the Association to adopt, even on an informal basis, because it is one which once again appears to be partitionist in its construction. The underlying implication is that where issues that might touch on Northern Ireland politics — such as Rule 21 — are concerned, the grouping of nine Ulster counties functions as a kind of satellite association within the GAA as a whole.

Despite all the lip service that was paid to the one-nation ideal, the decision to retain Rule 21 was giving tacit recognition to the fact that there were two separate political and administrative entities on the island of Ireland. Those Ulster counties opposed to the lifting of the ban were more than ready to accept this because it allowed them to dictate the agenda and decide the pace of change. But it paid scant regard to the views held by GAA members in the other twenty-three counties.

The political situation in Northern Ireland has traditionally given Ulster representatives a considerable degree of influence in the GAA, and it was accepted that their views would override those of anyone from outside the province. This was the way in which the GAA had done business for a generation and it was an approach informed by pragmatism of the highest order.

However, it was also one more example of the way in which the GAA's internal politics and organisation were so inextricably tied to the *Zeitgeist* in Northern Ireland. Valiant attempts may have been made to hide this overtly political dimension to the GAA's day-to-day workings throughout the Troubles, but it rose repeatedly to the surface.

The blunt instrument that was Ulster's block vote ensured that Rule 21 was not a live issue in years immediately after the ceasefires. Without Ulster's lead, the GAA mandarins in Dublin were never likely to take the initiative; the inaction of the status quo was allowed to continue. That mood was transformed, however, by the Good Friday Agreement of 1998.

The deal that was salvaged from what seemed like inevitable failure was predicated on an understanding that the political and cultural life of Northern Ireland had to be reconstructed. The Agreement challenged prejudices and questioned the fundamentals of the old way of doing things. In the wave of optimism that followed the Agreement there was a feeling that almost everything was now in the melting pot and that conditions were ideal for forging some new ideas and a new way of doing things. Everything, it seemed, was up for grabs.

Joe McDonagh, the incumbent President of the GAA, certainly viewed it that way. The Agreement was made just weeks before the 1998 Annual Congress, and the GAA could not escape the breathless pace of change that was running through Irish society, north and south, during that frantic time. The GAA, however, appeared to have little room for manoeuvre, as no motion to remove Rule 21 had been set down for debate at Congress since 1995, and none was on the 1998 agenda.

Nevertheless, as Congress unfolded on 18 April, McDonagh picked up the ball and ran with it himself. Rumours had been circulating around Dublin's Burlington Hotel, the Congress venue, that the President was poised to announce a major policy initiative in relation to Rule 21. As the morning progressed, these rumours were met by rumblings of implacable opposition from the Ulster delegates, who quite forcefully made the case that the President had, as yet, no mandate for removal of the Rule. They argued that any change should be postponed until a clearer view of the emerging new political landscape could be obtained. Bubbling below the surface was the old tenet that, without Ulster on board, Rule 21 should remain in place. The

Ulster delegates made it known in no uncertain terms that, if the President was now attempting to jettison the rule unceremoniously, they reserved the right to stage a very public and potentially embarrassing walk-out from Congress.

This was something that Joe McDonagh and the GAA hierarchy were determined to avoid at all costs. The President made a rapid assessment of the situation and made subtle changes to his approach. In a powerful address he made it clear that he felt the time for removal of Rule 21 had now come. However, to obviate the impact of the forces of opposition ranging against him, he announced that the matter would not be dealt with at Congress, but would instead be the subject of a special congress on 30 May. He had bought himself some time and averted a split. It was a very GAA way of doing things.

Nonetheless, the Association excelled itself when it reassembled the following month. Having used the intervening period to take soundings, President McDonagh was left in no doubt about the invidious situation in which he now found himself. Ulster delegates were telling their President and anybody else who cared to ask that they felt abolition was a course of action which they considered both over-hasty and ill-advised. While now publicly yoked to a policy of abolition of Rule 21, McDonagh was confronted with a significant rump, possibly even a majority, within the GAA who vociferously opposed that same policy.

At the special congress, Joe McDonagh made all the right noises about the GAA recognising the need for change and its willingness to play its part. But even his skilful rhetoric was not enough to paper over the cracks. The two-thirds majority needed to pass any motion seemed unattainable, and the issue was never put to a vote. Instead the congress unanimously adopted a resolution that committed the GAA to deletion of Rule 21 'when effective steps are taken to implement the amended structures and policing arrangements envisaged in the British–Irish agreement'.

This splicing together of abolition with RUC reform did not happen by accident. Rather, it was a clever piece of politicking by McDonagh's opponents who had enough foresight to see that policing was always likely to be one of the most problematic elements of any permanent peace settlement. The passing of time was to vindicate that assessment. Running parallel to this, the commitment to remove the rule and the positive nature of the statement went some way to assuage the reformers and to blunt media criticism.

One commentator sagely described the entire process as the elevation of unity over principle, and there is no doubt that the Rule 21 debate holds up a revealing, warts-and-all mirror to the modern GAA. In particular, it shows that the Association is no closer to the formulation of a coherent, consistent approach to events within Northern Ireland than it was thirty years ago.

Throughout the Troubles the GAA had seemed to construct policy on the hoof, maintaining always a reactive rather than proactive presence. Little wonder then that when that political violence began to shake down after the ceasefires and the Good Friday Agreement, the GAA was similarly leaden-footed.

The cobbled-together compromises of early summer 1998 bought the GAA some time, but it was always clear that Rule 21 was going to be the focus of a lot of attention as the Commission on Policing in Northern Ireland, chaired by Chris Patten, began its work. Once again the GAA was cast as one of the main political actors in the debate that grew up around the issue of RUC reform. The existence of Rule 21 was always likely to be advanced by some elements to counterbalance clamours for reform to the RUC name or badge. The removal of one, it was suggested, would be a *quid pro quo* for the removal of the other.

In the event, when the Commission's report was published in September 1999, the GAA featured at number 114 of the 175 proposals contained in it. The recommendation was succinct and to the point:

> The Gaelic Athletic Association should repeal its Rule 21, which prohibits members of the police in Northern Ireland from being members of the Association.

The message could not have been more clear. But the GAA took some solace from the fact that the recommendation was also in line with the Association's commitment to removal of the rule as enunciated in May of the previous year.

The full text of the Patten report, however, provided much more food for thought, and moved the entire debate forward into much choppier waters. At 15.2 of that text there was a recommendation that 'all community leaders including sports authorities should take steps to remove all discouragements to members of their communities applying to join the police and make it a priority to encourage them to apply.'

The recommendation for repeal of Rule 21 was then followed by a further observation.

> The continued existence of this rule in the light of our recommendations can only be a deterrent to the recruitment of Catholics, or a factor in separating those Catholics who do join the police from an important part of their culture.

The resonances for someone like Seán McNulty were obvious and it was clear that the Patten Commission was expecting the GAA to go far beyond the largely cosmetic exercise of a redrafting of its rule book. The element of 'encouragement' envisaged — that the GAA should play a role in promoting membership of the police force as a good and positive thing for its members — was going to require a seismic shift in attitudes that had not yielded for generations.

There was also uncertainty. How far was it expected that the GAA would go in satisfying the recommendations? Would club officers put up recruitment posters on dressing-room walls or provide membership forms? Would police officers from any new force be invited into GAA clubs to speak to under-age players and enlist potential recruits?

The simple response was that nobody knew and the GAA was not about to go out of its way to provide any quick and easy answers. The Association's now-familiar tactic was to allow the dust from the fall-out of Patten to settle and adopt a wait-and-see approach. This was greatly aided by the seemingly interminable rows that surrounded the implementation of the Patten proposals as a whole. As debate raged around issues like the name of the new force, its badge and its uniform, the GAA kept its collective head down hoping perhaps that Rule 21 would quietly fade from view.

Unsurprisingly, that didn't happen. Rule 21 continues to hover around the business and workings of the GAA, unloved by most but clung to by the many members of the Association who are decidedly unsure about what the future politics of Northern Ireland may hold. Seán McCague's elevation to the Presidency in April 2000 was not expected to bring with it any radical policy shifts. Seán McCague is from Monaghan, and, as an Ulsterman, is well tuned-in to mind-sets and thinking within the province.

Nevertheless, just before assuming the presidency, McCague made a speech to the Monaghan county convention, in the course of which he suggested that it would be the Ulster counties that would have to lead the way in any movement towards repeal of Rule 21. Those comments were predictably seized upon, but in the rush to dissect them McCague's caveat that all this could happen only at 'the appropriate time' was overlooked. It was clear, therefore, that while he was allowing room for manoeuvre, the fundamentals of the policy position of May 1998 had not changed.

And so it seems likely to continue. The GAA is more than content to allow the debate about the future of Northern Ireland policing to rage around it. If and when the new structures are in place, it will respond. Such a response would mark the end of the most controversial political issue in which the GAA has been involved throughout the thirty years of the Troubles. But until then, Rule 21 remains the unwelcome ghost at the GAA table.

*

Despite all the procrastination and dragging of GAA feet, Seán McNulty feels that the end is in sight. As he sees it, a commitment to abolish Rule 21 has been made, and it is now a question of how long it will take for that to be implemented.

> It hasn't been done away with up until now but I think it's only a matter of time before it is done away with. Hopefully.

Hopefully. I think they'll make the right move. It would be nice to see life return to normal up here.

As someone who is away from all the wrangling over procedure and policy positions, he introduces a human dimension to the occasional hostility of the ongoing debate.

I've known policemen who did play Gaelic football before the bans were strictly adhered to and they spoke about it regularly to me. They should have been playing right through all of this. A blind eye was turned before the Troubles and they were never really at risk until it all really kicked off.

Seán McNulty has a young family of his own now, and his enduring desire to immerse himself in the GAA burns as brightly as ever. With change seemingly on the way, that goal is closer now than it ever has been and he is excited at the prospect.

Certainly. Why not? I'd love to get involved at club level again. Before I joined the police, going back maybe twenty-five years, I was running the under-12 and under-14 teams. It was great and I would love to go back and do some sort of coaching at underage level. That's where my heart is because there is just so much talent there. I would be quick to spot somebody's potential and that's something I would miss out on. Coaching would be great.

Circumstances dictated that none of that was conceivable during the Troubles. But Seán McNulty now looks forward to introducing his own son to everything he left behind.

I'd love to see him playing Gaelic football. And hopefully if things progress I'll push him on into playing for the school and then for the club. A few years ago it would have been very difficult for somebody like me to take kids to the GAA club and then collect them again. But now things are going the right way and you can relax a bit more and plan for things like that.

Seán McNulty is looking forward to that future. The past is a different country.

Chapter Six: The Field

As deliverance days go, 3 April 1999 was a strange, subdued occasion. The Crossmaglen Rangers club in south Armagh was hosting a fairly nondescript National League game between an Armagh county side that was on an upward curve and a Leitrim team in fairly serious decline. It was Easter Saturday, and by throw-in the crowd had swelled to a few thousand holiday-weekend onlookers. There wasn't much to get excited about. Even the man from local radio on the open-topped lorry that doubled as a press area at the side of the pitch was not his usual ebullient self. This was a game to be endured as much as enjoyed.

As the game wound its way towards the preordained Armagh win, a half-whispered rumour began to circulate just before half-time. Somebody had been talking to somebody else. And that person had been listening to the radio news on the way to the game and heard a short report about the British government handing back the Crossmaglen ground to the club. The news swept around the ground but was greeted with weary scepticism rather than wanton celebration.

In keeping with the way Crossmaglen and its officials had been treated over the preceding thirty years, nobody from the government had contacted the club.

'I think the mood was muted, funny enough, after such a long fight,' remembers long-serving Crossmaglen official Eddie Hughes.

There was just a recognition that it had to come sooner or later and we hadn't really gained anything. All we had got was our own land back. There were no parties or anything and no free drink at the bar.

But it was deliverance all the same.

*

Rightly or wrongly, the fate of Crossmaglen Rangers GFC had become inextricably bound up in the way in which the GAA had manoeuvred itself through the thirty years of the Northern Troubles. More than any other single factor or event, the treatment meted out to the club by the British authorities had forced the Association into the political arena. GAA officials found themselves attending high-level meetings with representatives and ministers from both the British and Irish governments, and it became clear that, after Crossmaglen, the GAA could never again affect the same degree of detachment from the realities of political life in Northern Ireland.

Unlike many of the injustices, perceived and otherwise, of the past thirty years, there was tangible, visible proof of the way in which Crossmaglen had been treated. And that proof could hardly have been more symbolic than the looming, hulking presence of the British Army sangar on one corner of the football pitch owned by the club. The technical term for the occupation of St Oliver Plunkett's Park was 'requisition', but that did little to assuage the resentment and anger among the local population.

Long before the British Army ever established a presence in south Armagh and long before the pitch became a potent political football to be knocked between the opposing interests, Crossmaglen had been a by-word in GAA circles for Gaelic football of the highest quality. Remarkably, that tradition has endured through everything and, as Eddie Hughes and another long-standing club member, Tom McKay, sit in the committee room of the magnificent new club complex on a cold February evening, the Crossmaglen men are on the cusp of another

All-Ireland club title. The roots that were set down when the club was formed back in 1887 have anchored everything, and since then Crossmaglen has won Armagh county titles — 29 in all — in every decade except the 1950s. Above everything else Crossmaglen teams are winners. Tom McKay says:

> I would say that the club is basically the community. The community revolves around Crossmaglen GFC. This parish of Upper Creggan is a hotbed of Gaelic football in the sense that we would have 1,450 families in the parish and we have three teams this year playing in the premier division of the senior league in Armagh and there's one team in intermediate football in County Louth. From fourteen hundred families that's some record.

To live in south Armagh and to play football for Crossmaglen was to be imbued with a sense of both place and identity. The club quickly became the means by which people in the area defined themselves and presented themselves to the outside world. Eddie Hughes says:

> Your identity would automatically become bound up in the club. Gaelic clubs exist on a voluntary basis and that voluntary basis is itself based on actual physical help in running teams and stuff like that, the financial side of things. So it has to be part of the community. This place here is used for birthdays, weddings and deaths, as well as entertainment on any other given night. Back in 1966 Mass was even said in the old place here when the chapel was being renovated. So we are part and parcel of the local community, always have been and hopefully always will be. It's no different, I think, to any town or village throughout Ireland.

What distinguished Crossmaglen from those GAA idylls in the rest of the country was its strategic location and the serious, ongoing security situation that developed around it. In 1975, Merlyn Rees, then Northern Ireland Secretary of State, coined the description 'Bandit Country' for the village and the surrounding area. But even without the Rees sobriquet, Crossmaglen was always a place set apart. Tom McKay believes this has created a very particular mind-set in the people.

> In this area people would consider themselves Irish without necessarily proclaiming it from the rooftops. We always

considered ourselves Irish because our natural hinterland is Carrickmacross, Castleblaney, Dundalk, this type of thing. Necessity would force people to go to work the 'other way', Belfast and Craigavon. And in the years they were building Craigavon they used to write poems about the ones who were travelling down to the 'big smoke' and that sort of thing.

This perception of themselves inevitably brought with it a political dimension for the people of Crossmaglen. It was a feature of the GAA club almost from its inception. According to Tom McKay:

> In the very early stages, the 1920s, there were splits in the clubs about politics. One side took the Redmond side against the other side. So there were periods of division, but eventually they would come back together again.

When this united front was presented, it faced predominantly in one direction.

> The outlook was basically Irish and I think Margaret Thatcher coined the phrase that only for a slip of the pen where they included the wrong river Crossmaglen could very easily have been in the South. We continually look South and we rarely look North. If we're going for a day out it's Dublin and it's rarely to Belfast. That has always been our philosophy. So once the Troubles came we were never going to allow ourselves to be pushed around.

Even in more peaceful times, GAA membership carried its own political baggage. In the occasional flare-ups of violence that characterised the forty years of life in Northern Ireland before the onset of the Troubles, the GAA was an obvious focal point. The events that unfolded during the 1970s and 1980s were nothing particularly new to Tom McKay.

> In the 1950s I was a member of a club in Newry at the time. We were coming from playing a football tournament in either Armagh or Keady and on the way home we were stopped by the B Specials on the Armagh Road and lined up and searched. And from then on there were regular occasions when you would be stopped, particularly by the B Specials. A policeman would be very formal but they would just be very rough with you. If you played Gaelic games or supported things Irish you were going to be looked on with suspicion.

*

Such unease was a constant throughout the 1950s and 1960s but the situation was transformed by the sustained political unrest and culture of violence that established itself in the late 1960s and early 1970s. South Armagh became — for want of a better word — a battleground, not just in military terms but also on a more elevated symbolic political level. The ability of the British government to control the area that encompassed south Armagh and, just as importantly, to be seen to be controlling that area, became one of the totems of the conflict. In that context, the Crossmaglen football pitch was catapulted into the national and international consciousness.

Given that it was soon to become a full-scale occupation, the origins of the Army's encroachment onto the club's property seemed fairly innocuous. The local RUC station had always stood just beyond the boundary wall of the land owned by Crossmaglen. It was originally intended to house just six policemen, but in the early 1970s it expanded rapidly to accommodate the huge influx of British Army personnel into the area. In May 1971 some of these soldiers began playing games of football on the adjoining pitch when they were off duty. The club protested; lip-service was paid to those protests and they were formally acknowledged. But the incursions continued.

As the year progressed and the political situation deteriorated, military activity in the area increased dramatically. The Army began using the pitch as a helicopter landing-pad as it had been adjudged too dangerous to transfer personnel and equipment by road. The timing of these landings was wholly arbitrary and occurred on many occasions when games were being played on the pitch. Players were forced to dive for cover.

Again protests were registered but, as the tension mounted, in wider political circles little notice was taken of the club's plight. It wasn't long before the intimidation was replaced by actual violence. On 17 May 1972 Silverbridge was due to play Crossmaglen. Just before throw-in a helicopter landed and soldiers emerged with orders to clear the pitch. Patrick

Tennyson was playing for Silverbridge that evening. Afterwards he said:

> There were about one hundred or more people on the pitch, which included players and spectators. One of the soldiers came down to where I was standing a little apart from the others and he said: 'I told you to leave the pitch.' As I was turning around to leave the pitch, without having spoken a word, he hit me with the barrel of his gun on the side of the face. I was dazed when he hit me, but walked then a bit further and after this I do not remember anything as I fainted. The next thing I remember was waking up in Daisy Hill Hospital.

Events had clearly taken a much more serious turn and the harassment continued away from the ground itself. Eddie Hughes and the other members found themselves confronted with numerous problems as they attempted to continue as a functioning GAA club.

> The classic example is that we were going to play a league match on a Sunday. The bus would leave from the club here. Players would get on the bus and as soon as you went to pull out the gate the soldiers would come out of the barracks and stop you. They'd ask where we were coming from and where we were going. And because they mightn't have got a polite answer or something like that — and even if they did get a polite answer — they'd keep you half an hour or three-quarters of an hour. So you would then arrive late for your fixture.

The fact that this was happening soon became widely known in Armagh GAA circles, and a collection of unwritten but rigorously observed rules sprang up. The most important was that, where clubs from South Armagh were involved, throw-in times were not to be rigorously observed in case of 'delays' en route. Teams were usually given an hour's grace, and the points would not be claimed. So, even if the Crossmaglen team bus pulled up at the home team's ground at a time when, anywhere else, everybody would long since have gone home, the game would be played. In the 1970s, the GAA in many parts of Ulster had to become adept at engineering these local compromises.

Around this time a cycle of correspondence began between the Crossmaglen club, the office of the Taoiseach in Dublin, and the Northern Ireland Office at Stormont; this was to continue for the next three decades. However, despite the club's protests, the Army activities continued.

A perimeter wall around the ground was demolished to allow easier Army access, and the surface of the pitch was repeatedly damaged by heavy machinery moving in and out. Between March and August of 1972 helicopters landed on the pitch when matches were in progress on five separate occasions. The situation was spiralling out of control and those in charge of the club were facing the very real prospect of losing all of their ground permanently to the British authorities.

The effect, says Tom McKay, was devastating.

> If you cast your mind back to when they took over here — the condition of this place — then it becomes clear. Players and supporters would have to be ferried up on the back of a lorry to the field here because the whole area was that cut up with their heavy trucks coming in and out and that sort of thing. It was knee deep in mud. When the club attempted to put gates on their premises they just brought out their big Saracens to knock the gates down. They just drove over them.

The pitch lost its status as a county ground because people were too afraid to travel to the area, and college games were similarly curtailed. Training and preparation became all but impossible; it seemed that the lifeblood of the club was being squeezed out.

Crossmaglen and its GAA club had become another front on which the battle for hearts, minds and territory within Northern Ireland had been opened up. The gloves quickly came off and the club found itself at the centre of some unwelcome public and media attention.

> There were newspaper articles saying that members of the committee of the club were sitting up here around a table at night, plotting the downfall of the security forces. The thing about that was there were a number of us who were civil servants. How was that going to help your prospects, never mind actually putting your life in danger?

And still the requisition orders kept coming. Eddie Hughes explains:

The order is served on you and that's it. It is signed by the Secretary of State and it actually means that you no longer own your ground. There is no comeback to it. That was part of our problem in terms of development because the requisition order ran right down the side of the clubhouse. And at one stage right out to the 50-yard line of the pitch was actually ploughed up by the Saracens and other machinery turning on it. There was very limited playing time on it at that time because a lot of it was just pure quagmire. All that is well documented.

In June 1974 the British Army took possession of a large part of the spectator area around the pitch, and again in November 1976 more land was occupied. By this stage, the GAA at a national level was beginning to take a real interest, and the situation in Crossmaglen had become part of the wider political debate.

The then president of the Association, Con Murphy, visited Crossmaglen in 1976 and issued a statement afterwards. Even twenty-five years on, it is still a remarkably trenchant piece of social and political commentary — all the more so when you consider that the words came from the pen of the most senior GAA official on the island. The statement read:

> I must truthfully say that I am appalled at what I saw and learned. The complete entrance to the grounds is taken over; entrance gates and fences are damaged; the GAA social centre is damaged and cut off, therefore unusable in the circumstances; and most important of all, about 30 yards of the playing pitch has been destroyed by heavy vehicles, thus rendering the playing field useless. Players and officials are being constantly harassed by the soldiers. In other words, the people of the area are absolutely deprived of their rights.

The president then went even further, describing as 'highly provocative' the stance adopted by the British Army. He left no one under any illusions as to where his sympathies lay.

> The local club officials and members, whose only anxiety is to preserve the GAA property for recreational facilities for the local community of all age groups, are to be admired for their courage, patience and sense of responsibility in these 'highly provocative' circumstances and our Association is in full support of their stand.

In the context of everything that followed in the twenty-five years since, this intervention by the highest-ranking official within the GAA hierarchy is extremely significant. This was the GAA rolling up its sleeves and getting involved in fundamental, grass-roots political issues in Northern Ireland.

The role of the GAA, and perhaps even more importantly, outsiders' view of that role, had been fundamentally redefined. The conundrum of Crossmaglen forced the GAA to shift from a reactive to a proactive approach. The ramifications of that are still being felt today.

At the time it was a sign that the plight of the club was not being ignored. From the outset, according to Eddie Hughes, the collective approach was unequivocal:

> We never confronted them or anything like that. There were confrontations by them, you could find yourself removed from the field at gunpoint when the helicopters were coming in. That continued right up to the early 1980s.

The alternative course of action had to be along diplomatic lines.

> We did have good support from Con Murphy. He set up a sub-committee — the Crossmaglen Croke Park committee — which dealt with issues concerning the club at that time. There was no contact or communication with the Army and they did as they pleased. All our protests were made through the Department of Foreign Affairs in Dublin. Probably only for that support we would have lost what we had left of the field. There were actually plans at one stage where the whole area was taken over for married quarters incorporated into the rest of the base.'

*

The situation surrounding the occupation of the Crossmaglen ground settled inexorably down into a grinding and draining war of attrition. On the field, the club continued to blaze its trail of achievement, winning three county championships during the 1970s, and two in the 1980s.

Outwardly, therefore, Crossmaglen displayed its familiar veneer of success. But twenty years on, Eddie Hughes is well placed to see the more fundamental and far-reaching effects of the long-running stand-off. Whereas previously Crossmaglen was an example to other, less progressive clubs around it, it has spent the past few decades playing catch-up.

> You have to remember that this club from the 1950s on was probably twenty years ahead of its time in terms of development and stuff like that. We had a county ground and a hall that could raise finances for the club — a facility that few else had at the time. But then when it came to 1970 and years after that we actually fell twenty years behind — clubs that had been twenty years behind us actually passed us in terms of development. So I believe that we lost out very badly on that end of the club.

Crossmaglen had to function on two fronts — on and off the playing field. Inevitably, something had to give.

> Most of our people's time and effort was actually geared towards securing that place. It was a full-time job going to meetings and arguing our case to hold on to what we had at that time, never mind the hindrances that were put in our way to actually developing anything because of the requisition orders that were served on the club. From day one it has been a long, hard, dour struggle right through just to survive. Not on the football field, but outside of the football field it has been a long struggle just to keep people interested.

Crossmaglen had always prided itself on being a GAA club that was about much more than merely playing the games and sending teams out to compete in the various leagues. The social and community dimensions of its work had always been just as important as the playing side of things. Eddie Hughes and the other club officials were forced to preside over a period of relative decline — the very fabric of Crossmaglen GFC was under attack.

> It affected the club and I'm sure there are other clubs that could say the same. The particular problem was the close proximity of the barracks on the premises. It's something that's always very hard to explain but there was always something underlying there, something hidden and it affected the morale of personnel within the club. It affected the performance of the administrative side of the club in terms of development and stuff like that.

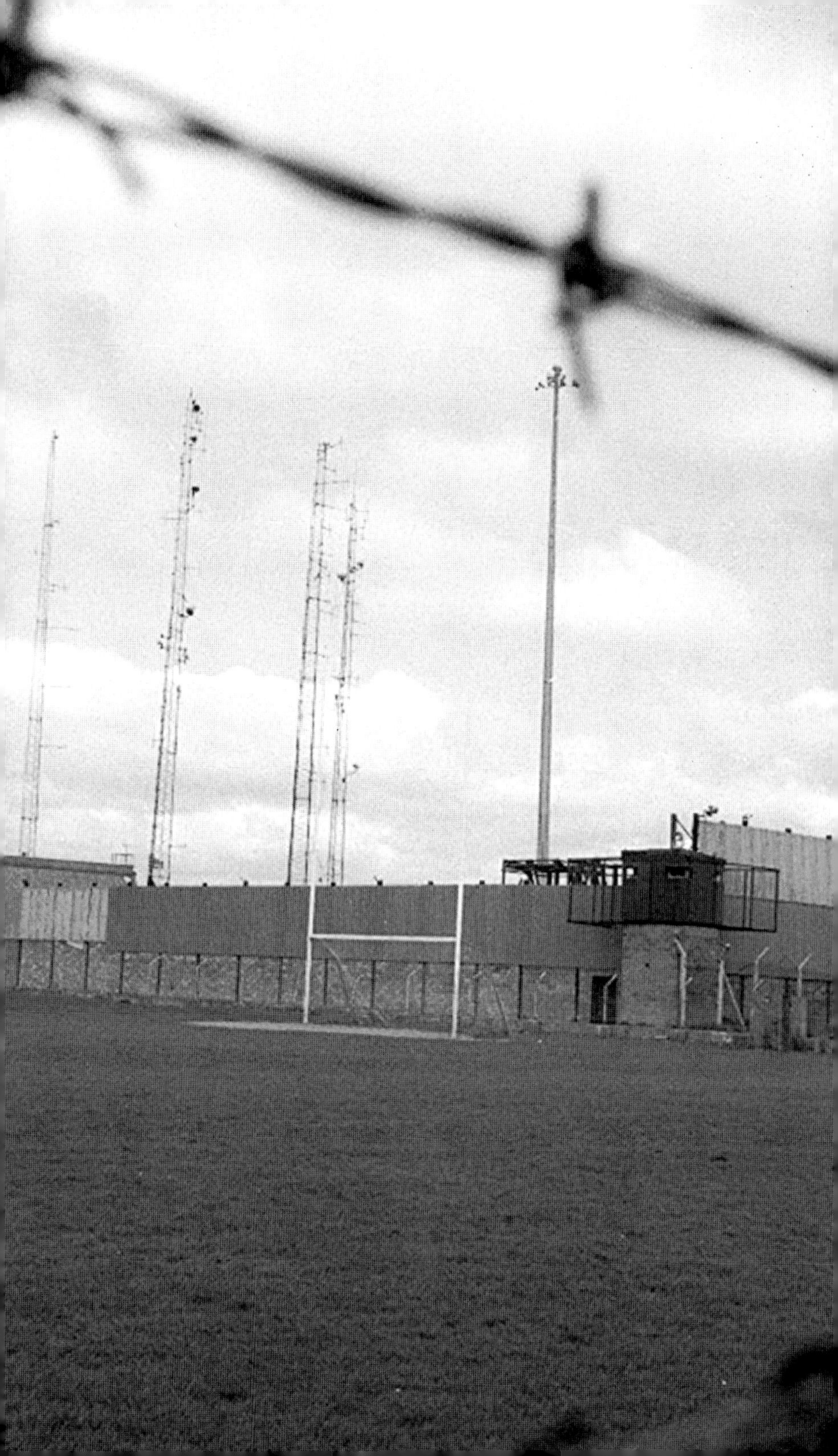

Above: The St Enda's under-12 team in January 1975. The two boys at either end of the back row, Gerry Devlin (left) and Liam Canning (right), were both killed during the Troubles. (Photo: St Enda's GAA club)

Below: The border checkpoint at Aughnacloy, County Tyrone, where Aidan McAnespie was shot dead on 21 February 1988. (Photo: Pacemaker)

Previous page: The British Army base looming over the Crossmaglen Rangers pitch in south Armagh became one of the most powerful images of the Troubles.
(Photo: Pacemaker)

Above: *The premises of Ballycran GAA club were attacked on numerous occasions but each time the members were determined to rebuild.* (Photo: Brendan McCarthy)

Below: *Aidan McAnespie: 'Despite everything that happened to him Aidan always remained very dignified.'* (Photo: Pacemaker)

Above: Seán Brown, abducted and murdered on 12 May 1997. (Photo: Pacemaker)

Above: Gerry Devlin, murdered outside St Enda's GAA club in north Belfast on 5 December 1997. (Photo: Pacemaker)

Above: Seán Brown's body was found beside his burnt-out car near Randalstown, County Antrim. (Photo: Pacemaker)

Above: The rapid growth of women's football during the 1990s gave the GAA an important new dimension during its most difficult period. (Photo: *Ulster Herald*)

Above: The 1981 hunger strikes and the accompanying nationalist protests represented a significant challenge for the GAA. (Photo: Pacemaker)

Above: *The scene of destruction after a bomb exploded in the centre of the County Tyrone town of Omagh on 15 August 1998. Many of the dead and injured had close associations with the GAA.* (Photo: Pacemaker)

Left: *Brenda Logue: 'She was the life and soul of the club'.* (Photo: *Ulster Herald*)

Opposite page: *In the aftermath of the Omagh bomb the GAA was confronted with a catastrophe of an unprecedented scale.* (Photo: Pacemaker)

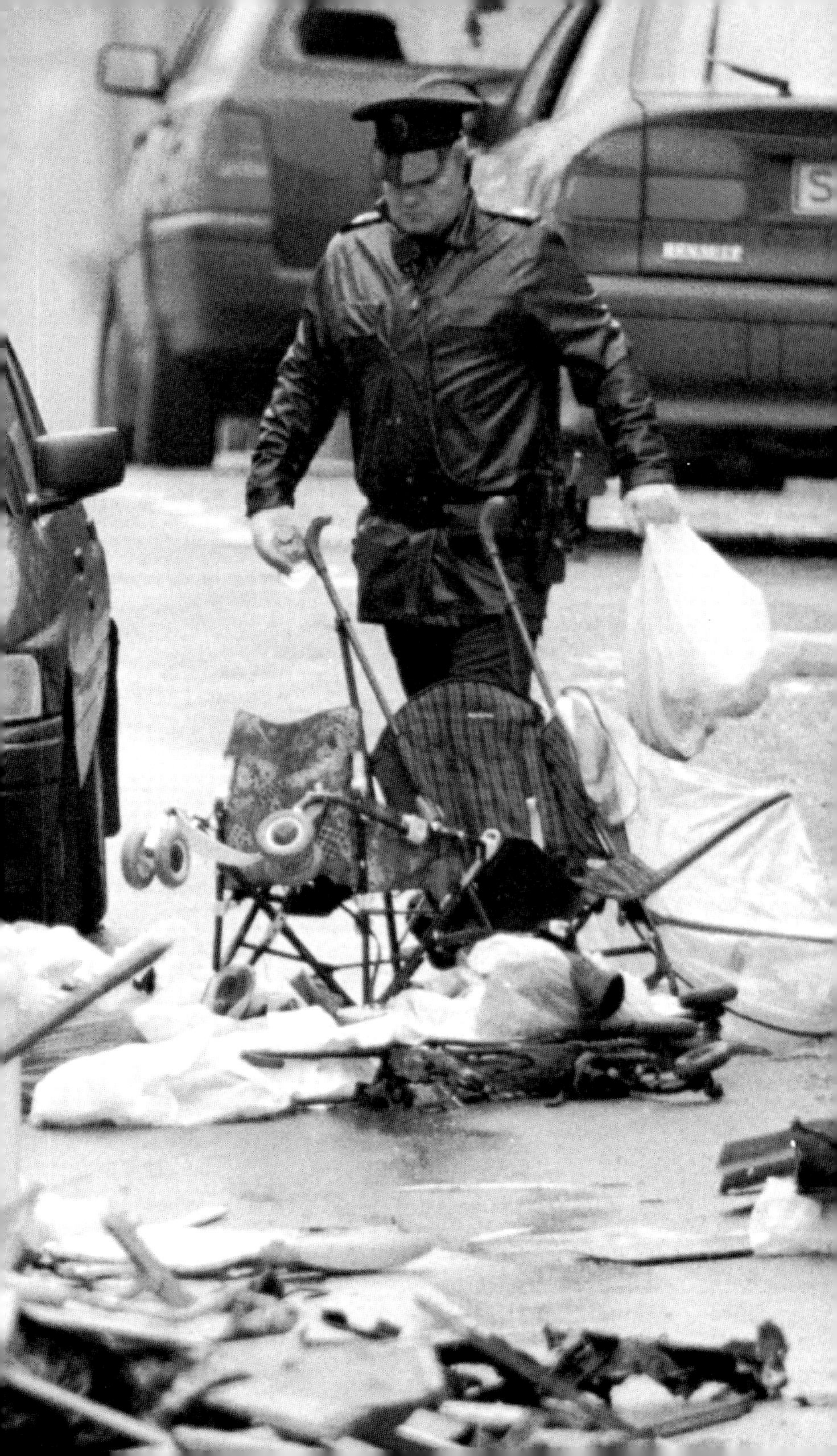

Above: *Noel Keith of Ballycran, Down and Ulster. Hurling and football survived and thrived in Ulster despite the worst ravages of the Troubles.*
(Photo: Ballycran GAA club)

Left: *Captain, Paddy O'Rourke, lifted the Sam Maguire when Down won the All-Ireland football title in 1991. Seán McNulty had played alongside him 14 years previously.*
(Photo: Inpho Photography)

Parents who had previously thrown themselves into the bread-and-butter jobs that keep a country GAA club like Crossmaglen operating — driving children to training, washing the jerseys, running the line or acting as umpire on Saturday mornings — drifted away. The constant threat of confrontation for anybody in the vicinity of the football field was the only disincentive needed. It was almost inevitable that the club would suffer. Eddie Hughes remembers:

> People were afraid to come openly to participate in the running of the club. They were happy enough for their children to come and they knew they were going to be looked after well but people themselves were hesitant to become involved, and the club lost out greatly on that. We were very lucky in that we probably had some of the best administrators within the Association belonging to the club. But, nevertheless, in terms of numbers, we lost out badly. I've always felt that.

There were constant practical difficulties for those who tried to keep the club afloat. A straightforward half-mile journey from Eddie Hughes' house might take half an hour and involve being stopped at four separate vehicle checkpoints, usually manned by soldiers from the base at the pitch. Committee meetings were interrupted regularly by the arrival of a group of soldiers who would walk around the hall and leave again, often without explaining their presence or asking any questions. The targeting of the club for this type of treatment was relentless, but there was a dynamic that meant the situation never became hopeless. Eddie Hughes says:

> It was never totally impossible, but it was always very difficult because of the problems you had getting new people involved. We were lucky in that we were supported financially by the community despite everything. But to do that you must have personnel to gather the money and put on functions to raise more. And we were lacking in that, particularly in the early years. Now, from the late 1980s on, most people got educated in a sense about the Troubles and were not as easily intimidated, so they came out more in support of the club. But in the early years it was very difficult and the club suffered greatly because of that.

That 'education' in relation to the Troubles was paralleled by a growing awareness of the club's situation at national level. The Crossmaglen Croke Park Committee, set up by Con Murphy, established itself as a powerful lobbying group and took some pressure off the club because it did not now have to deal directly with the authorities and government officials.

The issue became a regular feature on the agenda at the GAA's Annual Congress; the passing of motions offering support and demanding that all occupied property be handed back was an indication that the Association was presenting a united front. This made it possible to move tentatively forward. High-level exchanges and meetings between GAA officials, members of the Dáil, and British government ministers were initiated, and, as the very worst days of the Troubles were left behind in the 1970s, the 1980s saw a slow shifting in attitudes. The first sign of a definite thaw came in February 1985 when the club went to court to recover compensation for the loss of income and amenity that stemmed from the occupation of their grounds.

The repeated position of the British government right from the time of the first requisition order back in the early 1970s had been that compensation would be paid for any loss suffered by the club. The difficulty was in translating that laudable principle into concrete action, and negotiations had been ongoing for years before the matter finally reached court early in 1985.

At the end of a long day's negotiation and deliberation over the exhaustive financial records it had been required to produce, the club accepted an offer of £150,000. The importance of that award went beyond mere money. It was an indication that further movement might be possible in the near future.

The club became emboldened by this prospect of change and began to formulate plans for a new dressing-room and social complex. The car park was also reclaimed after years of use as a right of way by the British Army. Over the years it had become abundantly clear that the fate of Crossmaglen Rangers was closely linked to wider political developments, and that any movement there would have to be counterbalanced by a parallel gesture elsewhere.

After decades of trying doggedly to remain in some way above the political process, the GAA found that it had become one of the main actors. The degree of involvement in the process increased significantly with the first IRA ceasefire in 1994, but Eddie Hughes and others realised that they were treading a fine line.

> At the end of the day, while the Association in general is not a political association or a political party, that is not to say that there are not political views within it and that members do not have the ears of politicians. We were lucky enough in that we had people in very strong positions who were sympathetic. They understood the position, they acknowledged that there was an injustice being done to a voluntary sporting club and they knew it was a wrong that needed to be righted.

Officials from the club worked hard to keep Crossmaglen somewhere near the top of a crowded Northern political agenda, and there was a continuation of behind-the-scenes efforts to secure the return of the occupied parts of the ground.

One of the difficulties was the overriding requirement that no party in the dispute could be seen to lose face, and it slowly became clear that the club was being shoehorned into a situation where the return of the ground had to be met with some sort of reciprocal gesture.

The form which that gesture should take soon emerged. The political situation in Northern Ireland during the second half of the 1990s was as fluid as it had been for a generation. There was a real sense that this was an opportunity to reshape some of the building blocks of the society in an all-embracing new political settlement. Policing and the future of the RUC were at the core of this, and the nationalist clamour for reform of the police force became one of the keynotes of the entire process.

It was hardly surprising, therefore, that somewhere along the line linkage was made between reform and the GAA's Rule 21, which prohibited members of the RUC and the British security forces from joining the Association. From there it was not a quantum leap to throw the situation in Crossmaglen into the melting pot.

For some, the temptation to connect all these ostensibly disparate elements became irresistible. This was a GAA club situated in the shadow of an RUC station complaining about injustices that had been meted out to it. And yet that same club was part of an Association which, as part of its official rule book, denied membership to those same RUC officers.

The Crossmaglen club found itself trapped in an invidious position where its complaints were being set against government and unionist unhappiness with Rule 21. It was a quid pro quo that club officials railed against vociferously and consistently. They refused to countenance any development of the debate which connected their situation with the controversial rule. Eddie Hughes says:

> I think the connection between the two was more or less the perception of some people but obviously we had no control over how people aligned themselves. The club's view was very simple — that our issue was a completely separate issue from anything else. It stood alone. The ground was occupied by the military and that was it, end of story. It had no relation to anything else, absolutely nothing to do with rules or any other political undertones.

Those connected with the club made no attempt to deny that its plight and the status of Rule 21 were both part of the fabric of the GAA, and that one might colour the other. Eddie Hughes' objection was to any attempt to equate the two and embark upon some kind of trade-off.

> Other people who maybe could have been swayed as to whether Rule 21 should go, I'm sure their opinions were certainly affected by the problems that were associated with Crossmaglen. There's no doubt about that at all. Even though we're saying they were two separate issues, other people may still have viewed them as one.

Given the club's location and the negative experiences of many of its members in the preceding thirty years, it was obvious that many people within Crossmaglen would take a certain view with regard to Rule 21. But, according to Eddie Hughes, there was unhappiness among members when that stance was represented as some kind of intransigent bargaining position:

> As regards Rule 21, the club's view has always been whatever the view of the Association is. If it's a rule of the Association, that's it, and if the rule goes, the club will acknowledge that — the club would have no problem with that at all. But if Rule 21 had gone, it wouldn't necessarily have made our case any different.

The first tangible signs of movement came with the election of a Labour government in Britain in 1997. Members of the club had a meeting with a group of Labour MPs and received a sympathetic hearing. The constant theme was that this was simply a situation where a sporting club was seeking the return of its own property. But Eddie Hughes had been led up enough blind alleys to remain cautious and pessimistic.

> You see, vague promises were always made and the vague promise was that the ground wouldn't be held a minute longer than was needed. But that was like how long is a piece of string. It could have been forever. All it took was for someone to say that it was needed and that was it. I suppose from 1998 there were undertones that there was movement afoot. There were political implications to everything at that stage but again our view was very simple. Because of the problems that we have had with them, we wouldn't believe anything that was happening until we saw it ourselves or at least saw it in writing. That was our view because they had made so many promises prior to that on different issues.

Even at this stage the club still had to cope with its situation being associated with the building momentum surrounding the whole issue of Rule 21. The GAA itself was culpable of joining the two issues at its annual Congress in April 1998.

As discussed in the previous chapter, in the aftermath of the Good Friday Agreement, the then President, Joe McDonagh, made an ultimately unsuccessful attempt to force through the deletion of the controversial rule. But in a move that was clearly designed to calm Northern jitters, the Taoiseach, Bertie Ahern, delivered a speech which suggested that movement on the return of Crossmaglen's land was imminent. The connection had been made yet again between what the club itself maintained were two separate, unrelated issues.

Away from the political horse-trading, bit by bit normality crept closer. The security fence that had encroached onto the pitch was moved back. A perimeter wall that had penned the club in was knocked down and moved out of the club's land and back within the confines of the barracks. The life of the club took on a more normal rhythm, and even though helicopters still flew low over the pitch from time to time, it was not on anything approaching the same scale as during the worst days of the 1970s. Everything was pointing towards a total withdrawal. Nevertheless, when the news reports began to filter through on that Easter Saturday afternoon in April 1999, they were greeted with a degree of careworn cynicism.

> What we said that day was that we certainly hadn't been notified. We had nothing in writing to say this was the case — as far as we were concerned it hadn't happened until we could see it. After that, all the land belonging to the club was derequisitioned on 9 July 1999. That's when we said we had our club back.

Twenty-eight years after the first incursions onto their property had taken place, the members of Crossmaglen Rangers had regained all the property and land that were rightfully theirs. Eight months later, in Croke Park, the club's senior footballers beat Na Fianna of Dublin to win their third All-Ireland Club title in four years and put down their marker as the best side in the history of the competition.

It was a triumph over adversity, a fitting tribute to all those who had struggled before them. And it was deliverance.

*

After almost three decades of struggle Crossmaglen Rangers are in the previously unimaginable position of being able to take stock and look confidently into the future. But the wounds inflicted over the past thirty years will take a long time to heal. While success on the field has produced a buoyancy and self-confidence, there is still a lot of hurt off it. Club treasurer Eamon McMahon is perfectly placed to provide an overview.

> There were ten or fifteen years of stagnation and a loss of morale within the entire club structures and personnel. And it took a long number of years to work back up to that again. The building of these premises where we're sitting now — that's the self-esteem back now in the last few years.

As he rakes over the history of his club, Tom McKay sees much to be proud of. Crossmaglen found itself at the epicentre of a period of political turmoil — a time when the confrontation between the British Army and republicans was extremely highly charged. And through all of that, Crossmaglen with its underage teams, its social events and the dedication of a vital few provided an anchor for the community around it. Regardless of what other structures were under sustained attack, the club and the GAA were a constant. The importance of that cannot be overstated.

> The club really was the stabilising factor and we filled the social need. Because of the Troubles and because of the dangers on the road at night and all the killings that were taking place, we couldn't travel north. So we really had to fend for ourselves and provide activities for ourselves. But I think really that made us stronger, it really made us take a good look at ourselves and look at the sort of things needed to keep our young people happy.

This social dimension to a sports club's work is not particularly unusual. The smallest cricket club in England or bowls club in Wales would pride itself in providing an outlet for the young people in its catchment area. But in south Armagh during the 1970s and 1980s the stakes were somewhat higher. Crossmaglen Rangers are justifiably proud of their achievements.

> It's a very proud record that none of our young people got into trouble right through the Troubles. As part of that I think the club was blessed with very strong leadership during that particular time. At the height of it we had the late Fr Moran as chairman, we had Gene Larkin as chairman, Gene Duffy, Eddie Hughes. We had good continuous strong leadership which ruled

the club with a very firm grip and kept things in order, and that kind of thing. But yet we were strong enough to stand up to all sorts of intimidation.

Around the Lough Neagh shore in Tyrone, in north and west Belfast, and in south Derry there were men and women like Eddie Hughes and Tom McKay doing the same sort of work throughout the Troubles. These were different times and cultural life outside the GAA was all but non-existent. The club was the means by which generations of young men and women defined their lives, shaped their value systems and prepared themselves for the real world off the training pitch and outside the dressing room. Without this outlet and without the thousands of hours of unpaid, selfless work by those who took it upon themselves to act as guides and mentors, the social toll exacted by the Troubles could easily have been much higher. But in the rush towards war there were many who could not see the cultural and political wood for the trees. It was left to men like Eddie Hughes to attempt to impose some type of order.

> That is one of the things that has always amazed me and that I could never understand. It's only relatively recently that the NIO and the British ministers — even the Irish ministers — would acknowledge the work that GAA clubs have done particularly during the Troubles of the last thirty years in places like south Armagh and Tyrone. It's only recently that they acknowledged the good work they actually did do during those times in providing for the youngsters and keeping them off the street.

There were times when it became a struggle to keep all the balls in the air at the same time. Tom McKay and others felt the pressure.

> That was one of the reasons that we went south to the Department of Foreign Affairs in Dublin with all our problems. We never got local politicians involved directly regardless of who they were or what they were and that was one of the reasons that was done. At club level politics was never mentioned and I would say without contradiction that politics never came into the day-to-day life of the club. The hunger strikes, for example, in 1981 was a very emotive time in nationalist areas and I think

the GAA stood very strong and very fair and guided the way through for everyone. It was definitely a time when things could have got out of hand.

The difficult thing for Eddie Hughes and others to countenance was that, in direct opposition to this, all the vehicle checkpoints, the helicopter landings and the house-searches seemed to be driving those same young people into the arms of republicanism

That's why I could never understand here about the obstacles that were placed in the way when we were trying to keep youngsters involved in something that was not political. Everybody would acknowledge that 99 per cent of youngsters who were in the GAA are not involved in destructive things within the community. They're not involved in trouble and they're not stealing or stuff like that. That is a fact. But what it came down to in the end were acts of intimidation and harassment of the club and of the people in general because it was seen as a nationalist identity, if you like. It was about keeping them down at all costs.

*

One of the by-products of the struggle that surrounded the occupation and eventual return of the Crossmaglen lands was the way in which it forced the GAA to become educated about itself and its place in the new political and social order of life in Northern Ireland. Before the Troubles the GAA position of non-political detachment was easily sustainable and was clung to stubbornly. But as the sparks of political violence were lit all over Northern Ireland during the 1970s, these old assumptions were challenged and toppled. Even if the GAA did not regard itself as an organisation with a powerful political and cultural dimension, it is abundantly clear that the British government and its security forces certainly did.

The positioning of the old RUC base right beside the GAA pitch in Crossmaglen may originally have been a geographical accident, but nothing which transpired during the twenty-eight years after it was occupied could be dismissed as chance. The targeting of the GAA seems to have been regarded as a means of targeting one of the core building-blocks of the local community. The timing of each incursion and each helicopter flight, and the positioning of each vehicle checkpoint left Eddie Hughes certain of this.

> It was an attack on the GAA and the people of the area. There's no doubt about that at all.

As a result of the persistent campaigning work of the Crossmaglen members and the annual airing of the issue at the GAA Congress, the Association found itself, almost by default, centrally involved in the political debate. The input over the years of officials from both the British and Irish governments copperfastened that position because after those meetings had taken place it was untenable for the GAA to present itself as merely an interested, almost dispassionate observer.

With its huge countrywide membership, the GAA was now an important political player, but anything as overt as outright support for nationalist or republican politics would have had catastrophic ramifications for its members. The GAA, therefore, had to perform a delicate balancing act between satisfying the demands for words and action from its own membership in relation to issues like Crossmaglen, while at the same time retaining an identity and integrity divorced from the worst ravages of the political violence in Northern Ireland.

For the most part it succeeded in this and the skilful way in which a low-level but doggedly insistent campaign for the return of the Crossmaglen ground was carried out is the best example of the wisdom of that strategy. However, the ultimate resolution of the Crossmaglen situation was, whether the club liked it or not, another strand in the political tapestry that was being painstakingly woven in the aftermath of the Good Friday Agreement. The incontrovertible wrong that had been done to the club with the incursions and eventual occupation back in 1971 was no longer part of the currency of the debate. And for the stuttering political process to continue, it was ordained that there had to be some form of reciprocation on the GAA's part. That was where Rule 21 entered the mix.

As the fallout from the Good Friday Agreement has continued since 1998 with one milestone after another being painstakingly reached, the issue of policing has remained as the most potent live issue. The shape and structure of any future police force has proved to be a hugely emotive issue. Rule 21 has not been at the centre of that debate but its spectre has continued to lurk around the fringes of it. The most significant thing about this is that it means that the GAA as a whole is a party to the ongoing discussions regarding policing and, as such, is politically involved in the way in which life in Northern Ireland is being reshaped and reconfigured.

*

Outside on a cold and uninviting February evening there is snow on the way, an icy bite in the air. Another training session for the senior footballers has finished but the floodlights along the side of the pitch still flicker through the enveloping darkness. All-Ireland club titles are notoriously difficult to come by and down around these parts they are under no illusion about the effort and the selfless dedication that is required. They are still walking the walk.

Downstairs the hall is busy with women organising and reorganising tables for a fund-raising dinner dance the following evening. They are fussing over seating arrangements with the same sort of attention to detail that has fuelled the success of the football teams. This is a club with a clearly defined ethos.

Many of the battles may have already been won but the hard, day-to-day work of keeping a successful GAA club functioning and thriving goes on. Crossmaglen Rangers GFC is potent and living proof of one of the founding tenets of the GAA — the tremendous collective strength that comes from a united community and how much can be achieved when that is channelled into its local club.

Crossmaglen has drawn on this not only so that it could endure but also so that it could prosper. The way it is now is the way it always has been.

Over the years and decades Crossmaglen has mined the rich seam of its football tradition and established itself as one of the pre-eminent Gaelic football clubs in the country. The walls of the clubrooms are papered with photographs of under-age teams going back twenty years, and of players and officials from over half a century ago. The haircuts are a little longer and the clothes a little less fashionable but the same names occur again and again: McConville; Kernan; Short; Duffy; Larkin — all part of the same shared tradition.

For any club to have achieved such a level of sustained excellence and success would be a source of great pride and wonderment. But all that is magnified a thousandfold when it is a club whose very property and future were under continual threat for almost thirty years. The rise and rise of Crossmaglen GFC is one of the most remarkable Irish sporting stories of this or any other era.

Chapter Seven: Outposts

The abiding memory of a midwinter's night on the Ards Peninsula is the unrelenting and unforgiving blackness of the place. As the road snakes south out of Belfast through Newtownards and then stubbornly hugs the winding shoreline of Strangford Lough, you leave the comfort of the streetlights behind you in the rear-view mirror. In their place there is only darkness and silence, and you find yourself gradually enveloped by a tremendous sense of isolation. Intermingled with this is an element of foreboding, the nagging feeling that you are leaving something behind and taking a few tentative steps into what is truly a place apart.

Brendan McCarthy's directions had seemed clear enough at the time. The secretary of the Ballycran club — one of only three hurling clubs on the Peninsula — has, understandably enough, become fairly adept at plotting the route for the legions of GAA people who have made this journey before me. His instructions were:

> Carry on out of Newtownards and go through Greyabbey and Kirkcubbin. Then take the first left when you see a sign for Clough and Portavogie. After that it's the first left again and you're at the club. It's less than a mile.

All of this had seemed fairly unambiguous at the time, and there was no indication that Ballycran's isolation, perched out there on the edge of the eastern side of Northern Ireland, was going to pose any particular difficulties. It wasn't as if it was that far away. Not a problem. But hastily scribbled notes are of little or no use when it's as much as you can do to navigate a way through the gloom and stay between the hedges. What should have been a short trip from Belfast was slowly but surely becoming a journey into the unknown.

Eventually the headlights illuminate the promised road sign and the relative comfort of what passes in these parts for the 'main road' is replaced by something altogether smaller and even more narrow. The lights from bungalows in the distance provide some welcome help with perspective as the car struggles up the hill. The first sign of journey's end grows progressively bigger on the left-hand side. The afterglow of a set of floodlights seeps weakly through the gathering mist, and another left-hand turn sweeps you up to the wrought-iron gates and the car park. Welcome to Ballycran.

The wheels of the car crunch on the gravel and drown out the shouts of the brave souls who are training with the Down senior hurling panel on one half of the nearby pitch. It is mid-January and cold. Bone-chillingly cold. These are hardy men, made of stern stuff. But anybody who was supposed to be here has already arrived and the noise of a strange car brings two or three men out of the warmth of the committee room to the door so that they can check that everything is all right. Experience has taught them to be wary of unexpected and unwelcome visitors in the dead of night, and old habits die hard. What they have is worth protecting.

*

Of all the ways various groups and individuals have found to express their antagonism and their insecurities in Northern Ireland over the past thirty years, arson still seems to be one of the most base and the most elemental. The very act of burning is so mindlessly destructive and ultimately so futile that it can be driven only by ignorance and hatred of the most fundamental kind. There is a very clear message at the heart of every act of arson — what we don't like, want or understand we destroy.

Even in periods of relative political calm, the burnings go on — Orange Order meeting places, Catholic parish centres, church halls — the litany seems never-ending. GAA clubs have also been on the receiving end, often caught up in a cycle of tit-for-tat attacks on Orange halls. Among the worst affected have been the hurling clubs on the Ards Peninsula, which have found themselves time and again to be easy, isolated targets for arsonists operating with the protection and anonymity of darkness. And so the men with burning and destruction on their minds have been regular, unwelcome visitors.

St Joseph's Ballycran has been targeted on numerous occasions, but three separate incidents when the clubrooms were burnt to the ground stand out in the members' memory. Each time, they drew on their small catchment area and relied on members' goodwill to rebuild. Those efforts drew on every available fragment of inner-strength and self-reliance.

In the space of one year at the start of the 1990s, and just as the political situation began its final stagger towards some sort of resolution, the club's premises were attacked and destroyed on two separate occasions. These were not random, haphazard attacks — this was a campaign of intimidation on an organised, well-planned scale.

For a long time it felt as if the clubs were under siege and all but forgotten. But in this most unlikely of environments, and against almost all the prevailing elements, hurling on the Ards Peninsula has survived and even thrived. If the endless pattern of firebomb attacks stands as a powerful symbol of the campaign waged against the GAA in the area, that survival is an even more enduring indication of the strength and courage of those who provide the Association with its backbone. These are hardy people — hurling people to their very core.

*

The history of the tiny hurling community on the Ards Peninsula is one of the more idiosyncratic stories in the GAA annals. The wealth and sheer volume of talent at the disposal of the hurling superpowers — the Kilkennys and the Corks of GAA land — are well documented. As the game's vista has expanded through the past decade with the arrival of counties like Clare and Offaly, the ability of those counties to survive and thrive within the strictures of only a small number of clubs playing hurling within their boundaries has been widely recounted.

However, all those apparent problems fade into near insignificance when compared to the situation in Down. The county's proud football history has made it one of the patricians of that code. But when it comes to hurling the county is still very much down with the common people. The football team draws its strength and inspiration from the heartlands around Newry and its fertile hinterland. These are areas that have produced generation after generation of some of the best footballers the game has known, and they have the All-Ireland medals to prove it. But in those places, with a few rare exceptions, hurling has never really bedded down to the same extent, and few players, if any, make the cut for the senior county panel.

Instead, generations of managers, selectors and mentors have had to channel their attentions to just three clubs, all within a few miles of each other, out on the Ards Peninsula. Ballycran, Ballygalget and Portaferry have been the life-blood of Down hurling right throughout the history of the game within the county. The import of that is fairly obvious — it means that in any given year the maximum number of players available for selection for the county side would be in the region of sixty, and, understandably enough, of those sixty, the subs and some of the less able players could swiftly be discounted.

That leaves perhaps thirty to thirty-five men from whose ranks attempts must be made to fashion an inter-county hurling team. That they have been able to do so is something approaching a modern sporting miracle — the GAA's answer to the parable of the loaves and the fishes. It is a constant struggle to continue to unearth new players, and hurling in Down has known some terrible times. And yet the family names echo down through the years — the Coulters, the Mallons, the McGrattans — and Down has earned the right to be spoken of with respect among the hurling counties of this country.

That respect is also bolstered by a universally held admiration for the dignity and courage with which the sport of hurling has been kept alive on the Peninsula in the face of what were, at times, fairly daunting odds. Drawing as it did on a small, quite self-contained nationalist community, the Ards hurling fraternity was always an obvious target at times of raised political tension. In many ways, the Ards men's struggle through that can be seen as a microcosm of the wider problems that the GAA has had to face down within Northern Ireland over the course of a generation.

*

For Ballycran there might not have been any hurling had it not been for the input of two men who arrived in the area over thirty years apart. In 1938 there was a new appointment at the local primary school when Frank McKenna moved from his home place in Scotstown, County Monaghan, to become headmaster. Sport in the townlands around him was never the same again.

The hurling bug had already bitten in the area and, unusually for Ulster, there was little competition from the sister code for the affections of the players. According to long-standing Ballycran stalwart, John Mallon:

> This was more or less a hurling area. There was no Gaelic football here at all. Ballygalget played a bit but it was only for three or four years because they just didn't have the manpower. Away back in 1922 there was a man called Harry Emerson from Portaferry who was secretary of the county board. Hurling was going very strong even then. They had three teams within that parish alone at that particular time.

But in Ballycran there were no such structures in place. Two local men — Hugh Gilmore and Pat Hamilton — looked on enviously at the way the game was thriving just a few miles down the road, and they made a decision that was to engender a fierce local rivalry that endures to this day. They would form their own club at home in Ballycran. Frank McKenna was to prove the driving force and, just a year after he arrived, the Ballycran club was founded — a testament to the pioneering spirit. According to John Mallon:

> They had been watching hurling being played in the south of the county and they approached the master here about starting a team and that's how it started in Ballycran. The parish then was only a thousand people and maybe only a hundred or less got involved within the club. But with the master at the school, he encouraged it at that level, and it took off fairly quickly. Within ten years, we had won a senior championship.

The production line was starting to roll.

However, in the early days, the team sometimes struggled for numbers. With Portaferry well established, and strong roots set down in neighbouring Ballygalget, the call for some help went out. It was answered in the form of three players from each of the two existing sides who played for a while on the new team and helped hurling to bed down. It would prove to be the high-water mark in relations between the clubs. In the years to come, things would get a little less friendly.

Master McKenna also looked further afield and drew on inspiration from all over the country. He was a close friend of the legendary Lory Meagher, a man who had been a mainstay on the great Kilkenny teams of the 1930s and, from midfield, had captained the county to an All-Ireland in 1935. So, as a tribute, McKenna decreed that the new hurling team would wear black and amber as a tribute to Meagher and Kilkenny. Those colours were an indication of the Ballycran desire to be part of the great hurling tradition.

Years later, the club would recognise the efforts of Frank McKenna by naming the park and playing facilities after him. It is an indication of the veneration with which his work is still regarded that even the road up to the field is now known as McKenna's Road. Without his influence and input, there might well be no Ballycran club.

In the early days, Ballycran fought hard to survive, and if there was success, it was also tempered by an ongoing struggle against the perennial problem of having only a small pool of players from which it could draw. The McKenna legacy was that hurling was the game of choice at schools level, but as some of the population ebbed away in search of work, it became difficult to keep numbers up: almost all the players were drawn from in and around nearby Kirkcubbin. Right on cue came salvation in the form of another outsider. John Mallon says:

> In this parish there would only be a certain number of people who would have been GAA-minded. That did create problems because it would be a drain financially on the boys who were interested. Then we had a curate who came here in the early 1960s, Father Connolly, and he injected new life into the club. He got a lot of the boys from the outlying areas to come and play hurling.

Ballycran was not all that unusual in this rather fitful hurling existence. Outside the one long-standing stronghold — the Glens of Antrim — the game in Ulster owes its survival to the contribution and persistence of outsiders. In many cases, as in Ballycran, these were members of the religious orders — Christian Brothers or priests, transplanted into Ulster from hurling nurseries like Cork, Kilkenny and Waterford. Like the first American settlers, they were horrified by the practices of the indigenous people — in this particular instance, their slavish devotion to Gaelic football. Nothing spurs a hurling zealot into action more than such agnostic behaviour, and these zealots quickly set about proselytising the GAA non-believers. Anything hurling that endures in Ulster today owes an immense amount to the evangelical work of those founding fathers.

What they could not have legislated for was just how quickly the arrival of the game in earnest would produce an intense rivalry between Ballycran, Ballygalget and Portaferry. If the Ballycran club owed a debt to those players who had arrived from Ballygalget and Portaferry to bolster numbers in the early days, that debt was soon forgotten.

For John Mallon the rivalry was a positive, even vital, element which contributed to hurling's survival and eventual flourishing on the Ards Peninsula. He finds it almost impossible to see where the motivation would have come from without it. As John sits in a cold committee room on a winter's night in January, he can still bristle at the prospect of summer and a resumption of normal service. He is a Ballycran man. Nobody can take that away from him.

> You just can't do without that rivalry. In fact, I would say that was the biggest factor in keeping hurling going in the Ards, that rivalry. Without that it would have been dead. That's my opinion. You just *had* to beat Ballygalget and you *had* to beat Portaferry.

In such a goldfish-bowl environment it was the other two clubs who provided the only worthwhile benchmark.

> If Ballycran went and painted their goalposts pink, Ballygalget would have had theirs painted pink the next week. What we did, they had to do.

Defeat was such an unpalatable prospect that it produced a communal depression that could go on for days; you could almost reach out and touch it. John Mallon played in enough of the games to recognise the caustic taste of defeat.

> If you were beaten by them, you maybe didn't look out for two or three weeks because you didn't want to meet them on the road.

His face still contorts into a grimace at the memory of it all. For the Ards men, this is more than just a game. With the stakes raised so high, the potential for confrontation was inevitable. In 1962 the situation reached crisis point in a Championship game between Ballycran and Ballygalget. John Mallon remembers:

> It so happened that it was a Portaferry referee. It really got out of hand, there's no doubt about it. The ambulances and everything were there. The fight was always there but the situation was calmed down with the opening of Portaferry secondary school in 1959. The boys from the clubs then all went to the same school, and that calmed it down a bit because before

that you just ignored the boys from the other club if you met them on the street. You just didn't talk to them. But it's a better situation now. You couldn't have gone on that way.

One of the unfortunate by-products of this often unfriendly rivalry was that the fortunes of the county side were subjugated to the greater good of the three club sides. Throughout the 1970s and 1980s Down remained in the hurling foothills and presented no challenge whatsoever to the one-party state that was the Ulster hurling championship dominated by Antrim.

Training was all but non-existent, and when the players did come together for a session before a big game, relations weren't much better. On occasion, the men from Ballycran would sit in one corner of the dressing room and the Ballygalget boys in the other. Not a word would be spoken between the two factions, and there would hardly even be eye contact before they walked out to take up their positions. John Mallon was among those who knew that something had to be done. Again, the influence of outsiders was to be pivotal.

> All the problems reflected on the field. If you were coming for a pass and they saw it was a Ballycran boy, they would maybe have passed it over that other way rather than give it to you. That was the way it was then. It was only there with Seán Holywood that we started to get a county team going into some sort of system, and then Seán McGuinness came in after that and he took it on from there. He inherited a good team and got a bit more out of them.

*

Problems on the field throughout the Peninsula were paralleled by the fraught political situation off it. The strength of the Ballycran club had always come from the people who had involved themselves in all the component parts that somehow fit together to produce a functioning GAA unit. The work had required dedication and effort, and there were times over the thirty years of the Troubles when that resolve was put to the test.

Right from the inception of the club, there had been a constant drive towards improvement, and a will to keep moving forward. The playing side was important and, with the local school firmly established as a nursery for the club, success soon followed. In 1974, Ballycran won the Ulster club title for the first time, and aspirations and expectations within the club moved up a notch or two. According to John Mallon, 'The big effect that had, was to generate a lot more interest in the game.'

Nevertheless, Ballycran was always about more than hurling. Its social position within the community was regarded as just as important, and much of the off-the-field energy was expended in that direction. The holy grail was the building of their own club rooms, and John Mallon and a whole generation of club members devoted themselves to that.

> These club rooms here opened on Christmas night 1969. It was all built voluntarily by club men. The ground had been bought in 1961, and the pitch was developed more or less voluntarily as well. That was finished by 1966 and they had a break of a few years before deciding that they needed to build a club room, community centre and changing rooms. The money was all raised by the club — I think it was something around £11,000, and it was all built with voluntary work. It's now insured for £350,000.

The prevailing culture which surrounded this initiative was markedly different thirty years ago. State support in the form of grants or Lottery assistance simply did not exist for GAA clubs on any significant scale, and when it came to improvements or development, it was a case of self-help or no help. Ballycran was just one of a multitude of GAA clubs where the men and women simply rolled up their sleeves and got on with it. The club rooms, halls and pitches that stand proudly in almost every parish throughout Northern Ireland are fitting testimony to their ability to get the job done.

However, this policy of state non-involvement also had its negative spin-offs. One effect of it was to create a 'them and us' situation, which served only to isolate the GAA and its members from the political and social mainstream. In the circumstances, it was hardly surprising that a siege mentality was allowed to develop, and echoes of that mentality survive today in the general scepticism towards the media and any other groupings which, it is imagined, are part of an organised anti-GAA establishment.

As the GAA developed during this period in not-so-splendid isolation, the forces of opposition were lining up against it. The self-help ethos at work in projects like Ballycran seemed to have an antagonistic effect on those already predisposed to be opposed to the GAA as a whole. The new changing rooms, the fine pitch and the popular community hall were symbols of a self-reliance that was viewed in some loyalist quarters as threatening. What followed struck right at the core of the Ballycran club and community. John Mallon says:

> It came out of the blue, the burning — 1974 was the big one. We were completely burnt out in 1974, and that was the first time. There had been a small attack just before that in the kitchen where they had broken a window and put a petrol bomb through. But that just happened to fall into the sink and didn't do a terrible amount of damage so then they burnt her down.

Even that was not the end of it as the attacks and the intimidation continued.

> After we got it fixed up again, they put another bomb in through one of the windows and burnt a big piece out of the floor. And during all that time as well, you had the bomb scares.

During that early part of the 1970s the political violence was at its height. The GAA had survived relatively unaffected, but the arson attacks and the petrol bombings on clubhouses throughout Northern Ireland had a cumulative effect. A general uneasiness was soon replaced by unequivocal fear. If the intention behind the intimidation was to make everyone feel vulnerable, regardless of their political or religious leanings, it was a chilling success.

> They had bombed the chapel and burned it to the ground the same year so everything that was nationalist or anything like that was a target. That was just it.

With a small, isolated population, and its location away from the much more visible centres of violence like Belfast and Derry, the Ards Peninsula survived the worst ravages of the early part of the Troubles. But the burning of the club rooms was a terrifying wake-up call for John Mallon and everyone associated with Ballycran.

> It came as a shock all right — you're damned right it did. It was only open three or four years and to see it in ashes was devastating around that time. The people were really gutted about it and that was on both sides of the community. The first man we had up to sympathise and see what he could do was Lord Dunleith. He arrived on the scene the next morning. The local Protestant people were annoyed about it as well. They didn't want the like of that happening here.

The most insidious effect of that first attack took a little longer to become apparent but it went far beyond the mere physical damage to the bricks and mortar of the Ballycran premises. Any early, innocent hopes of getting a foothold for hurling in the parish were swept away and replaced by a wariness and suspicion. John Mallon could see a lot of the old confidence draining away.

> It created a bit of fear in that you had to have security on all the time. We had to get security systems in the hall. At that time you couldn't really have come to the hall on your own. You know, if you were coming to open up, you nearly always had to have somebody with you. We didn't really know what was going to happen. It was a bit scary at the time, there's no doubt about that.

Club members became more conscious of outsiders and of their vulnerable position so near to the predominantly Protestant town of Newtownards, and beyond that the loyalist areas of east Belfast. As the years went on, they settled into an uneasy calm but were constantly aware of the possibility of further danger. Even the most mundane of club activities took on a much more serious aspect.

> If we had a function on or anything like that, the police would have kept an eye on the place, driving round and that sort of thing. We were all right with the police — they didn't bother us and we didn't bother them. They did their job and that was it. We had a couple of boys down over the years from Newtownards to talk to us about security, but as they said, if anybody wanted to come to bomb the place, there's damn all you can do about it.

Everything about the Ballycran club around this time exuded vulnerability. Although outwardly it operated in the same way as a GAA club might in Wexford, Waterford or Wicklow, just underneath the surface it was utterly different. The GAA in Northern Ireland had ceased to operate and function in the same way as on the rest of the island, and the awareness of that quickly became acute. John Mallon says:

> No matter what security we had as a GAA club here, they would always be able to do it if they wanted badly enough to do it. That's the way it was.

When the club ventured out of its local area, there were also difficulties. The paucity of clubs on the Peninsula meant that the three senior teams played in the Antrim leagues, where there was at least the possibility of some top-quality competition and the opportunity to hone skills. This meant travelling considerable distances for away fixtures, through areas where players and officials often felt vulnerable to attack. In the end, their ability to continue playing in Antrim was a triumph for pragmatism but it was never easy.

> To get a game of hurling we have to travel 50 or 60 miles at least, and if it is to north Antrim that's maybe 70 or 80 miles. One of the things about those games was that we have to travel through what would be considered very loyalist areas — the Newtownards Road, Dundonald. And when the Troubles were bad, there was a switch from travelling by bus to cars to make ourselves less obvious. We had our own bus up to 1987 but we did away with that because it was just too obvious. We were never actually attacked, but at the same time, looking back, it was risky enough.

The hurling survived somehow. Experience has taught the players that few things come easy, that progress is hard won and should be protected and carefully nurtured. The small hurling community on the Peninsula immersed itself in the game, and it became one of the life-forces for the area. Adversity had only made them stronger.

The optimism and drive of men like John Mallon were important. They kept their eye on the wider picture and were acutely aware of the implications that any collapse in the interest in hurling might have. This was not just a struggle to keep a pitch open or to send teams out to play in the league and championship. This was a fight for survival itself. The alternative could not even be contemplated.

So, when the fire engines and RUC investigators had long disappeared after each of the arson attacks, Ballycran set about rebuilding. It was hard to walk through the ashes and the charred rubble of each incident and confront the stark evidence of what had been done, but the club's members used those experiences as sources of strength. Each time they rebuilt, and each time they drew on the support of hurling people everywhere. The struggle became something they could turn to their advantage. John Mallon explains:

> I think people were maybe keener and wanted to show them by getting it back up again. There was no doubt that we would come back again. Kilkenny were one of the counties who came up when it was burnt; we had temporary mobiles which we used as changing rooms, that sort of thing. And we still trained here right through.

However, John Mallon also knows that something was lost in all of this — the wide-eyed optimism of sixty years before. The schoolmaster and one or two enthusiastic locals starting a hurling team from scratch became little more than a fading folk memory. It was replaced by a new scepticism and suspicion, a feeling that it was better always to be on your guard and prepared for the worst. This lingered long after the debris had been cleared away and the hall and changing rooms had been restored. The arson attacks had engendered a loss of innocence.

> There was a bit of fear, no doubt about that. You were always watching if a stranger came in a motor. You had to be vigilant because it would be dark when you were training in the months of January and February. The lights would be on at the pitch but in the dark out here you just wouldn't know who was driving in. You had to be careful.

After that first arson attack there was no going back to how it had been before. The Ballycran premises were to be targeted on numerous occasions over the next decade — 'other wee attacks', as John Mallon euphemistically refers to them. While nothing was on the scale of the devastation of 1974, the drip-drip effect of one attack after another left the club under siege. There were numerous unsuccessful fire-bomb attempts, and on another occasion the committee room was burned and badly damaged.

As with most forms of intimidation, the threat and the possibility of something happening were just as potent as the actual use of physical force. The lulls between attacks would be punctuated by campaigns of hoax bomb warnings, all of which were designed to instil a sense of uncertainty and unease in the club members. They were also clearly designed to cause maximum disruption. John Mallon recalls:

> Then there were those bomb scares. There was this one one Sunday here when Down were supposed to be playing Carlow. But we got a warning and so the game had to be transferred to Ballygalget and we played there.

And so it went on. Deep down, everyone knew that this was not a normal way for any sporting club to operate, but still they tried to preserve some semblance of normality. Through it all, they never lost sight of the fact that, above everything else, the games were the thing.

As the concentrated and heightened violence of the 1970s faded from view, the battle and demarcation lines within Northern Ireland were firmly established. The murders and the arson continued, but on a dramatically reduced scale compared to those darkest days. Life on the Ards Peninsula settled down into an uneasy calm. The heightened security steps that had been taken would never be enough to deter the most determined bomber or arsonist, but they did go some way towards allaying the worst fears and anxieties.

Ironically, day-to-day relationships between the Protestant and Catholic communities in the area were never particularly poor. The sense of difference between the two never receded completely but, as with many communities outside the polarised city environments of Belfast and Derry, there was a degree of tolerance and accommodation. There was also a realisation that, beyond all the disputes over territory and symbols, life still had to be lived in one way or another, and in the long term it would be better if this could be realised with the minimum of confrontation.

Nevertheless, the hard-line rumps remained on both sides. Within certain sections of the loyalist community, the perceived threat of a body with the membership and cultural influence of the GAA never wholly receded. And so, even though there were long breaks between the attacks on Ballycran and the other Peninsula clubs, that vista of intimidation never disappeared totally. John Mallon agreed that for much of the time it seemed as if the whole area was being targeted relentlessly.

> Yes, and that was because they attacked the other two clubs as well. They got the works too. We were all very easy targets out there on our own, and not very far away from some very loyalist strongholds.

With the luxury of a little distance, John Mallon can now see just how serious the situation in which they found themselves really was.

> I think there were two things. We were GAA clubs and they were close to us. I suppose it was the symbol they were attacking more than anything else. The place could be bombed and the people away in five minutes. And we are isolated here; before you could get any alarm raised or anything like that, everything would be gone. The good thing was that there was never anyone harmed — it was always done in the middle of the night and we were never actually attacked when there was anything going on at the club.

Meanwhile, the political landscape around them was changing, albeit very gradually. By the start of the 1990s there was a dawning realisation in the wider society that a continuation of the violence would ultimately be both futile and morally bankrupting. Minds turned, therefore, to the possibility, however remote, of moving towards some sort of settlement.

This had the important effect of reducing the levels of everyday violence as the endgame hovered into view. But it also meant that the confrontations were then opened up on other fronts, most noticeably those of culture and symbolism. This explains why the issue of loyalist and Orange marches became such a live political issue during the 1990s, and remains a major controversial issue, with no apparent sign of long-term resolution. The justification for these marches, particularly in areas which would have considered themselves predominantly Catholic and nationalist, was repeatedly questioned and so-called flashpoint areas emerged all over Northern Ireland. Protests became regular events in themselves.

For the organisers of the parades and their participants, this was tantamount to an attack on their culture and identity. Some believed that such attacks needed a counterbalance, and the obvious target was the largest cultural group associated with the Catholic and nationalist community — the GAA.

Despite its best public efforts, the GAA's pre-eminence within its own heartlands and, by extension, in Northern Irish culture as a whole, meant that it could not escape or avoid the wider political debate. If Orange marches were a cultural issue, so too was the position of the GAA. In Ballycran the attacks on the club started again. According to John Mallon:

> It had definitely died off for a while. We had nothing from the 1970s right through into the 1980s — no attacks at all. Then it started again in 1991 when they burnt us down to the ground again. A gas cylinder was toppled in through a window and on to the stage. The cylinder exploded and blew it up. After that there was just the four walls standing, nothing else.

The old cycle had re-established itself, and Ballycran reacted in the only way it really knew.

> So we rebuilt. We had her fixed and going again and were up and running within a year. The paint hadn't even dried when they burnt her again in 1992. That second burning was tough because it was sickening for us — to see the state of the place after it had been nicely done up and was operating again. But we survived it all.

The club once again tried to fall back on the old values of self-reliance and the pooling together of labour and resources.

But events took a decidedly sinister twist. The way in which the rebuilding process had quickly followed on almost as a matter of course from each debilitating attack had not gone unnoticed, and a loyalist threat was issued against anyone working on projects at GAA clubs or halls. The threat was ostensibly a blanket one against what was termed the 'pan-nationalist front'. But the hurling community on the Ards Peninsula was under no illusions, understanding that it was directed specifically at it.

The target had been broadened beyond the GAA buildings to the GAA people themselves, and that raised the stakes considerably. Personal safety became a priority. John Mallon fixes on this time as perhaps the worst of the entire Troubles:

> I worked on the hall myself the second time. And while we were doing it, it came on the radio that anyone working on GAA halls or anything that had been built were prime targets. We were putting the floor down one day and we looked up. There was a policeman just standing at the double doors with a machine gun. It near scared the life out of us. We didn't know who he was — he didn't have a cap on him or anything like that.

The rebuilding work went on but at a cost. There were some who were simply too frightened to continue both for their own safety and for that of their families. So they fell away and were lost to the club.

> After that day with the policeman, one of the boys who was with me went away and he never came back. That was the end of him. We can laugh about it now, but it wasn't a laugh at the time.

Like Crossmaglen and many other clubs across Northern Ireland before and since, Ballycran was confronted with a number of stark choices. All of these were predicated on one question — were there enough people within the body of the club who felt it was worth saving? This was never asked directly in the days after that second burning in 1992, but it was a looming presence in the background of everything that was being said or done.

Subconsciously, the decision was made to continue, and the training and the playing started again. That was the difficult part. After that, everything else was easy because, with the hurling taking care of itself, the club could rise again and prosper. The response of the players set the tone and dictated the future mood of the club. They provided the backbone for a golden period of success for the club. Ballycran came out the other side of its difficulties both stronger and with a toughened resolve. John Mallon believes:

> The boys really rallied around at that time and did a lot to get things back. They kept the playing end going too, which was important. We won another three county championships and another Ulster club championship around that particular time. It really got them together.

It was a time when they needed all the friends and support they could get. Newspaper and television interest was particularly intense as well, as both the domestic and international media latched on to a story that managed to combine sport and politics and provide an easy-to-understand snapshot of the effects that Northern Irish political conflict could have. The traditional GAA way when confronted with this degree of interest had been to retreat hastily back into its shell and wait for everything to blow over. The seam of media mistrust ran and continues to run deep within the GAA, and relations have generally been difficult and strained.

However, as the telephones began to ring and the requests for interviews started to pour in, John Mallon and the other seniors members of Ballycran decided to use it all to their advantage. At a time when there was a real danger of broader community interest and support slowly seeping away, this was a means of keeping the club in the spotlight and proving that it was attempting to rebuild and move forward. It was an imaginative and novel approach that was to reap rich dividends. John Mallon says:

> There was an awful lot of publicity. We even had people over from Japan — they came all the way from there with a camera crew. And we were happy enough with that coverage. Any GAA club should take all the publicity it can with things like that, and it was our way of showing all the work we were doing with the community. It was a way of showing that we were keeping going as well.

It was also a time when Ballycran became extremely aware of its place within the wider GAA community. As one of the outposts of hurling, seemingly cast adrift from its power bases further south in places like Kilkenny and Cork, Ballycran might occasionally have believed itself an afterthought. But when the members needed support most, it was there in abundance, and the club has been considerably enriched as a result.

> Jack Boothman was the President then and he came up a couple of times. There was also support from other clubs. We had a lot of donations from clubs and counties who took it on themselves to send us cheques. And there were Protestant people who sent us cheques for maybe £20 or £25 as a gesture of support. None of it was a whole lot of money but it was a gesture and a way for them to show support and say they knew what had happened to us.

Those many small acts of generosity, kindness and simple goodwill will never be forgotten. Their effect went far beyond mere finance — they were proof that Ballycran would not have to struggle alone. At the time, that was the most important thing of all.

The rising tide of the peace process since that low point of the early 1990s has been important for Ballycran. The threat of imminent attack has receded dramatically, but GAA clubs in other areas have remained targets, particularly at times of increased political tensions. The memories of the aftermath of the arson attacks are still raw, and club members remain fearful that they might have to go through the same experiences in the future. If anything, the cultural dominance of the GAA has increased in the past decade, thanks to enhanced television coverage and corporate sponsorship. Yet, GAA clubs in isolated, rural, mixed areas remain as vulnerable as ever.

Ballycran may be enjoying a sustained period of relative calm, but elsewhere the burnings still continue. The arson attacks are most prevalent in areas like south Antrim where solutions to the ongoing problems of identity and cultural accommodation remain as elusive as ever. And it is the very destructiveness of the burnings and the resentment they engender that makes the possibility of movement so remote. GAA clubs are still cultural battlegrounds, and their significance still resonates across Northern Irish society.

However, like Ballycran, the clubs continue to rebuild and keep the faith. The Ards Peninsula functions as a template and an example of what can be done in even the most hostile circumstances. In Ballycran, the dividing lines between the club and the community have now been blurred to such an extent that it is difficult to decide where one ends and the other begins. They feed off each other and both are stronger and more confident as a result. According to John Mallon:

> The club is simply the centre of the parish. This place is used for weddings, funerals, everything. Nearly anybody who has a funeral in this parish — the tea would be here after the funeral. The hall is used practically every night of the week as well — bowls, badminton and all that — and by both sides of the community. People from the other side come here and there are no problems at all.

The same indomitable spirit that saw Ballycran through those dark days is still needed to keep the hurling alive. The players set themselves punishing standards, but the club's survival is perhaps the greatest triumph of all. Sometimes it feels as if the members are always destined to struggle. All they can do, though, is keep looking to the future and all it might bring.

> Since the Troubles have finished, we're more relaxed about everything now. But sure, you never know, you never know. But the hurling will be here. At youth level, it's very strong here, both hurling and camogie. But you do lose a lot of players over the years — boys who have moved away to places like Belfast because of work. You really need young blood coming through onto committees, and young fellas looking after juveniles. But it will keep going here all right — no problem at all that way.

There is conviction and certainty in John Mallon's voice. There is no room for doubt or a lack of confidence. Ballycran has been through too much to let it all slip away now.

Chapter Eight: Handing on the Torch

Seán Brown was good with his hands. Everybody knew that. During the day he taught metalwork at Ballymena Training Centre and introduced students to the finer points of mechanical engineering. Always turning his hand to something, always willing to pass on what he knew to others, Seán Brown was a respected teacher, a man who always had something to give. His enthusiasm carried most of his students through.

Seán Brown worked in Antrim, but every day he came back to Derry. Leaving Ballymena, he would drive down the M2, turn right off the main Belfast to Derry road, and from there it was just a few miles into the village of Bellaghy. Home. The heart of things.

Gradually the boundaries between work, home and the local GAA club, Bellaghy Wolfe Tones, became blurred. On those journeys back from Ballymena, Seán Brown would be thinking of the jobs he could be doing at the club, improvements that could be made. His mind never stopped ticking over. It was just little things but it was the sort of attention to detail that had made Bellaghy Wolfe Tones such a pre-eminent force both on and off the football field throughout Ulster and Ireland.

So, he got involved in making the flagpoles that still stand guard over the pitch on the outskirts of the village. Then it was all the signs on the walls and doors inside the proud new club-rooms that had been rebuilt after a loyalist arson attack. It was never something he was asked to do. Nobody ever needed to ask him; he was a GAA man and this was just something that was part of him.

Later, he would have to turn his mind to some of the harsher practicalities of GAA life in Bellaghy during the worst years of the Troubles. The burning down of the club-rooms, first in the 1970s, and again a decade later, had been indications that the club was and would continue to be a target for loyalist violence. And so, when the decision was made to install security gates at the entrance to the sports hall, Seán Brown took on the job. No one was surprised — that was Seán all over.

However, the apprehension and the nervousness didn't go away. Having finished the security gates and supervised their installation up beside the club-rooms, Seán Brown began work on another set. These were altogether more imposing, fashioned out of wrought iron. Their purpose was to secure the car park and the entire club premises, right down at the junction with the Castledawson Road. It was difficult, intricate work but they too were finished and installed with the same trademark attention to detail. They helped people to feel just that little bit safer. Seán Brown had done his bit.

Just after half past eleven on the night of 12 May 1997 Seán Brown drove through those gates, stopped his car and went back to lock them up for the night. As he moved towards the gates — the same gates he had helped to make with his own hands — he was attacked by waiting loyalist gunmen. Seán Brown's body was found about an hour later, just across the border with Antrim, near the village of Randalstown. His burning car was nearby.

*

Seán Brown was good with people. His son, Seán junior, comes back to this again and again as we sit talking about his father in the front room of the family home. He tells a story that captures something of his father's character and reveals the void his death left, both in his family and in his club. It is a story that has been told many times with affection and love.

> I remember one year Jack Boothman, the GAA president, was the guest at the club dinner. Everybody was sitting down and we were just waiting on Jack. Daddy eventually had to go upstairs to the hotel room to chase him up and he was just lying in bed in his boxer shorts. Daddy was in a panic but Jack's attitude was that there was no rush. Daddy just wanted everything to run smoothly.

The Brown house is in the middle of Main Street, right in the centre of the village. Open the front door, take a step out, and you're in Bellaghy. The gap that separates the Brown family from the village and its people is barely discernible. And so it has been with the GAA club ever since they started playing in Bellaghy back in 1939. Inevitably, there was a Brown — Seán's father and Seán junior's grandfather — involved right at the start.

> A lot of the people from Bellaghy were actually playing for other clubs — Lavey, Toome, Ballymaguigan, Castledawson — in the surrounding areas. Basically around fifteen men decided to form Bellaghy club. There was a priest at the time who wanted to call it 'St Mary's' but they decided on 'Wolfe Tones' and that's what stuck.

Jim Brown was one of the pioneers, and the GAA began to course through the family veins. In the sixty years since the new-born Bellaghy Wolfe Tones emerged blinking and uncertain into the GAA world, the family link has been unbroken. As is so often the way in country GAA clubs with a small catchment area for players and an even more limited pool of available office-bearers, Jim Brown moved in and out of committee jobs over the years. He served as Treasurer several times, and in the early 1970s inveigled his son to join him as Assistant Treasurer. Handing on the torch — it was a pattern that was to be repeated with his son and grandson.

After those early days, the club soon established its position as a dominant presence and a defining force in this small country village. As GAA minds turn increasingly to the urban sprawls of Belfast, Derry and numerous other mushrooming towns, it is easy to lose sight of the all-pervasive influence that GAA clubs exerted in places like Bellaghy.

In the same way as the Brown house blends seamlessly into the main street, so it was impossible to say where the club ended and the community began. All village life of any substance — football, hurling, Irish dancing, concerts, bingo, socialising, drinking — found a focal point in the GAA club. To be part of that was to be part of the life of the village and vice versa. There were no boundaries.

Seán Brown junior remembers growing up in that comfortable cocoon. The GAA has been part of his life for as long as he can remember but it was never something that he was forced into. This was osmosis rather than force-feeding.

> That's one thing about Daddy — he never pressurised us into joining the club. He just let us follow our own path really. When we were younger and he wasn't really involved with the club, he wasn't going to put pressure on us. I remember that Tommy Diamond came and asked me to play under-12 football. I suppose I was one of the bigger ones. He asked my father first and he said that he would be better to ask me himself. Daddy wasn't going to say anything.

There were three other boys in the house and they made their way along the same path. James played when he was younger, but is troubled now with bad knees. Damien retired two years ago, while Martin also played when he was younger. That left Seán.

> I had been playing and then I suppose my father pushed me into the Treasurer's job. And I'm still the Treasurer of the football club today.

Carrying on the family line.

*

In the early years, the small group of founder members of the club might well have wondered whether all the hard work and effort were really worth it. There were lean times as they tried to establish themselves in the hard-bitten world of league and championship football in Derry. The first success was a decidedly modest one — a winter league win in 1947 — and it wasn't until a decade later that the club won a county championship.

After that breakthrough, the production line cranked up in earnest and turned up a succession of footballers who were amongst the best Derry had to offer. Seán Brown tutored his family in the GAA way of things during a rich period of the club's history. That element of continuity, not only in the Brown family but in a handful of other families in the village, has proven to be the bedrock on which all the subsequent Bellaghy success has been built. The remarkable thing is that the achievements have owed so much to the contribution of just a few families.

> They had that golden era between the 1960s and early 1970s when they were winning nearly every year or every other year. The team won the All-Ireland club in 1972. There was another championship in 1979 and then again in 1986. There was another lean period until the early 1990s and then we got to an All-Ireland club final again.

These were the salad days for Bellaghy, filled with joyous, lung-busting training sessions at the field on warm summer evenings and journeys up and down the county, laced with anticipation as they took on all comers. More often than not, Bellaghy ended up winning. But with the success came a sapping of some of the earlier enthusiasm. Gradually it became more difficult to get men to take on the jobs and the tasks that helped glue together all the different parts of the GAA club. The same diligent servants were still there; it was just that the workload was increasing all the time. Something had to give.

Seán Brown was immersed in bringing up his family and, says Seán junior, his interest waned just a little. He hadn't been involved in the nuts and bolts of the club for a while, but he couldn't stay away too long. Sooner or later, all the bonds and the ties would pull him back, because the GAA club had wormed its way into the fabric of the family life of the Browns. Seán Brown remembers:

It must have been the early to middle 1980s when he got involved again. They knew that my father had been Treasurer before so they came and asked him again. He talked it over with Mummy and decided to do it. And he was there until his death — as either Treasurer or Chairman.

The return of Seán Brown coincided with an important time in the history of the club. As confidence in the status of the GAA and relative economic prosperity became more apparent, clubs increasingly turned their minds towards the building of new, improved premises for their members. Dressing rooms and facilities were an obvious priority, but the exigencies of the political situation also led to the emerging trend for social facilities to be provided alongside.

During the political violence of the Troubles, hotels and pubs had become easy and obvious targets for paramilitaries, and attacks were regular occurrences. Often these were random and indiscriminate, resulting in an enveloping climate of fear. One solution was for organisations like the GAA clubs to take the initiative and build their own social centres and clubhouses which could be used for discos, dances and all sorts of social functions. The notional *raison d'être* was that the clubs could then exert some control over the situation and address the issue of security. The fact that these new facilities would provide some additional revenue was a welcome by-product.

Bellaghy Wolfe Tones proved to be one of the forerunners in all of this, and its social centre and sports hall were soon the envy of the county and beyond. When there was work to be done Seán Brown rolled up his sleeves and got on with it. The legacy of his tireless efforts during those early days still endures.

> When there were people who didn't want to take responsibility, he took it. It was basically from him that the social club was developed and he basically established the whole thing. And it was his idea to separate the social club from the football club, just to show that they were two separate entities. It has been like that since and I'm sure it'll be like that long after I'm gone.

It was as if he had never been away. Seán Brown once again immersed himself in the club and immediately gained respect from everyone with whom he came into contact. The social and financial side of things required a particular kind of drive and application, and Seán Brown proved to have these qualities in abundance.

> He was the type of person that was always able to get his point across without actually having to raise his voice or raise a rumpus. He was always able to approach the matter in the right way. If somebody was in a bad twist, he was able to get around them. He was always able to get people to do work for him by just asking them to do it.

Seán set himself the task of ensuring that the structures were in place off the playing field to mirror the success of Bellaghy's many teams on it. After he had eased the club through the early teething stages, he was able to get involved in the things he really enjoyed. It was almost as if a large part of him had been subsumed into the life of the club, and his son has fond memories of those times. Nothing that has happened since can take those memories away.

> When he started the Treasurer's job, a lot of his time was spent getting the books into his own way of doing things. Once he'd done that, the pressure was eased off and he was able to get more and more involved as regards different bits and pieces. He had that knack of getting people to do things for him and then he was turning bits of metal himself and making things for the club. It got to the stage where the keys for the hall were kept here in the house, and they're still kept here now. I have responsibility for them now.

*

Bellaghy is a name and a place which resonates with the history of the Troubles. Tensions flared regularly during the worst of those years, and both communities experienced intimidation, violence and even murder. The village was propelled into the national consciousness during the hunger strikes of the 1980s. Two of those who died during that protest — Francis Hughes and Tom McElwee — were from the local area. The village also became a familiar flashpoint for controversial loyalist marches long before the contentious parades became such an issue in local politics.

The local GAA club found itself in the same invidious position as scores of others at the time. Its members were victims of circumstance and, at times, it wasn't altogether certain that they wouldn't buckle under the strain. The pressures were there for all to see. The young men and women of each locality felt that they were on the receiving end of persistent and unrelenting persecution by a system and a state to which few of them owed allegiance. The difficulty was that they could find nowhere to turn, and so the GAA club, which had been the dominant sporting and cultural force in their lives since their earliest days, became an obvious focus.

Many of the protests that were mobilised in support of those on hunger strike and their campaign for recognition of their political status were yoked on to the GAA club in the town or village concerned. The clubs placed death notices in the obituary columns of the local newspapers; their appearance in the days after each hunger-strike death was black-and-white proof of their involvement.

The Bellaghy club had become well-versed in the art of survival in this political maelstrom. With nationalist politics in a state of ferment right through the early part of the 1970s, new ground rules were being set down. One imagined scenario in republican circles was clearly to utilise the established structures of the GAA clubs as a springboard for more concerted political activity. On the face of it, Bellaghy's large Catholic population and traditional nationalist and republican bent would have seemed like prime territory for an initiative like this to flourish. All the raw materials appeared to be in place and the well-established structures of the GAA club provided a ready-made framework. All it needed was the goodwill and support of the local people.

However, any moves in this direction were resisted strongly within Bellaghy GAA circles. The club, in fact, went even further than might have been expected, seeking accommodation for the disparate views within it, while at the same time remaining true to the ideals of the Association. Seán Brown provided the template. The Brown family had its own ideas about the way things should be done and these were passed down from one generation of servants of the club to the next. Seán junior says:

> The rules of the GAA say that it is a non-political organisation, and my father and my grandfather upheld those beliefs. Their attitude was that it was non-political and the club shouldn't get involved.

While this was laudable and worthy in theory, the practice proved to be more problematic. Bellaghy's position in south Derry, and, by extension, in the Mid-Ulster area, meant that it found itself right at the centre of one of the geographical focal points of the Troubles. The region was as notorious as south Armagh or north Belfast in the annals of thirty years of the conflict in Northern Ireland, and was the location for some of the worst violence of that period. During that time, the Bellaghy club and its members found themselves under considerable pressure from all sides.

> I'm sure there were a lot of scary times. This place would have been regarded in Northern Ireland as a republican area. I don't see it as that. There may have been paramilitary activity around the area but, to my knowledge — and, I know, the knowledge of my father — they were never able to recruit and grab that foothold in Bellaghy. There were enough people here who didn't care one way or another what happened and just wanted to be left alone. They didn't get involved. Of course, there were nights when Sinn Féin asked for the hall to run events, and they were given that. But that has not happened at all in recent years.

The importance of this stance in shaping the social fabric of present-day Northern Ireland cannot be overestimated. It is not hard to imagine a scenario where the GAA in areas like Bellaghy might bend under the pressure and effectively become a conduit for violence and paramilitary activity. The consequences would have been catastrophic, not only for those GAA people who got involved, but also for those who remained outside. They would automatically have become targets and would have found themselves sucked inexorably into the maelstrom.

In 1972, Bellaghy won an All-Ireland club title, beating UCC in the final. The names on the teamsheet were drawn from the familiar football dynasties of the village — Cassidy, Diamond, Brown, Quinn — but the most incredible aspect of what was already a fantastic achievement was that it came during the bloodiest year of the Troubles. More people — 496 — died during 1972 than in any other twelve-month period before or since, and the year was further marked by the deaths of thirteen civilians in nearby Derry during Bloody Sunday, and the devastation of Belfast during Bloody Friday.

Taking all that turmoil and upheaval into account, Bellaghy's All-Ireland victory is nothing short of remarkable. Seán Brown junior believes that football and the GAA provided an outlet and an escape at a time when everything else in the immediate hinterland seemed unremittingly bleak.

> That All-Ireland came at the beginning when there was maybe the worst killing. And I think the football at that time lessened the fears of the people around this area and made them look elsewhere rather than directly at the Troubles. They focused their attention on something else. I think maybe the young boys saw that Bellaghy was doing well and just wanted to get involved.

However, that level of interest brought problems. Sectarian murder, in all its terrible randomness, had become a fact of life during 1971 and 1972, particularly in the mid-Ulster area. Even the shortest and most mundane of journeys was fraught with difficulty. Somehow, Bellaghy managed not only to keep fielding teams, but also to prepare a senior version which was good enough to take on all comers from throughout the country, and to win.

> During the day it wouldn't have been too bad, but at night people didn't really want to travel. One good thing was that Bellaghy would have been playing in a lot of south Derry competitions and going to places like Lavey, Castledawson, Newbridge, Ballinderry — all of which you could get to without travelling through any real strongholds of loyalism.

But what I have always thought around this area is that while there are some people who are bigoted, a lot more on both sides are honest and decent. Even during that time I think a lot of people felt like that.

The success of the club helped it to tap into that goodwill, even during the darkest days. Ultimately, it was a means of self-preservation, and relations with the Protestants in the immediate Bellaghy community area have always been good. Any violence that was visited on the club came from outside. A willingness to embrace the virtues of sporting ecumenism is another quality of which Bellaghy GAA people are justifiably proud. Seán Brown junior can trace the roots of that quality back a long way.

There was a Protestant man who played for the team in the early years, called Sands. He actually did goals for them. There are Protestants who've actually shown an interest in the club as well. Most of the shop-owners in the town would be Protestants and people from the club would always have bought from them, so we never had any problem that way. When Derry won the All-Ireland in 1993, the cup came to Bellaghy one day and one of the first people I saw taking a photograph of it was one of the Protestant shop-owners.

During all those years, Bellaghy Wolfe Tones, with Seán Brown and others steering a path, was more than a GAA club. It performed numerous social and cultural functions and provided a framework and support at a time when many of the surrounding structures of society were under fierce and concerted attack. As in south Armagh and parts of Belfast, there is a feeling that, without its input and influence, the effect of the Troubles on the local community might have been much, much worse. According to Seán Brown junior, who was himself growing up in the village and with the club at this time:

The GAA club gave young fellas something else, something to look at. That then meant if the IRA was looking to recruit from around this area, there was still the GAA club for those fellas.

Right through this difficult time, the lead given and the example set by Seán Brown had established him as a prominent and influential community worker. His teaching work at the

Training Centre in Ballymena had brought him into contact with a generation of young people. The influence that he had on them and the skills that he passed on have endured after his death, and will be put to good use long after the men who killed him have themselves died.

Seán Brown lived his life as he would have had others live theirs. Throughout, he remained true to the tenets and the principles of the Association to which he devoted so much of his life. There was no place for bigotry or sectarianism of any kind, and he never allowed his love for the GAA to be coloured, tainted or blighted by them. This was ecumenism in the purest sense of the word, and it found its most vivid and lasting expression in the ceremony that Seán Brown organised to celebrate Seamus Heaney's elevation to the position of Nobel Laureate for Literature in 1995.

Seán Brown and Seamus Heaney had grown up in the same part of south Derry and were of a broadly similar age. Heaney's poetry is grounded in the land and the places around Bellaghy, and is a celebration of the way in which those surroundings have moulded and shaped generation after generation. Seán Brown saw much of himself in that poetry and would have been intimately familiar with the places and the people Heaney celebrated in his poems.

Seán was the inspiration behind plans to mark Seamus Heaney's achievements back in his home place. The obvious and only place to stage the ceremony was the Bellaghy club rooms, but Seán Brown was determined that it should be one of those rare events in Northern Irish society — a genuinely cross-community occasion.

> After Seamus Heaney had won his Nobel Prize for Literature, the club decided to honour him because of his achievements. Daddy was one of the driving forces behind it. And he went out of his way to make sure there were Protestants in the hall that night. He had gone out of his way to make sure it was cross-community. It showed the depth of damage the people that killed him did because it showed the extent to which my father had gone. He was a very well-known GAA person and yet he had crossed the divide.

The presentation made to Seamus Heaney was of a painting of a local landmark, Church Island, on the shores of nearby Lough Neagh. Like the Nobel Laureate, his countyman, Seán Brown, never lost that fundamental sense of place.

*

Thanks to the direction and leadership of the members, Bellaghy Wolfe Tones eventually came through the other side and surmounted the very worst hurdles set up by the Troubles. And while the spectre of political violence did not disappear completely, the severity of the situation did ease as the early part of the 1970s was left behind.

These were interesting times for the GAA as clubs, formed in flushes of enthusiasm thirty or forty years previously, began to mature and impose themselves on their more-established rivals. Bellaghy continued to be a powerful force at league and championship level throughout Derry, and the unity and sense of purpose that ran like a rich seam through all of the teams, from senior right down to the under-12s, became something that was both revered and envied. The vision of the early Bellaghy pioneers had been spectacularly realised.

Meanwhile, football at county level within Derry was on a rising tide. The quality of its under-age sides had never been in doubt. The county won an All-Ireland minor title in 1983 with Bellaghy man Damien Cassidy on the team. In 1989 the trick was repeated, with Karl Diamond from the club involved. The portents were good and the push towards a senior title began in earnest.

In 1993 Derry moved through the Ulster championship with a steely sense of purpose. Seán Brown loved it. This was a great time to be alive, to be part of it all. Three Bellaghy men — Cassidy and Diamond from the minor sides and Danny Quinn — were all on that 1993 panel, and the club could stand up proudly and point to the contribution it was making to Derry's collective good. It was a reflection of Bellaghy's strong standing within the county, and Seán Brown basked in the afterglow.

As the All-Ireland semi-final against Dublin and the final against Cork loomed, Seán Brown went into overdrive. Seán junior remembers it all as a bit of a blur.

> With the hype around that stage, there was just such a clamour for tickets. My father was in the middle of all of that and he was just in his element. He always tried to get everybody happy with tickets. If people had two tickets for separate seats away from each other, he would have got them together, that sort of thing. He had that kind of rapport with everybody.

On a September afternoon in Dublin, it came to pass that three Bellaghy clubmen walked up the steps at Croke Park to receive All-Ireland medals. Derry football had scaled what had always seemed an insurmountable peak, and the club had done everything that was asked of it. But still there was no let up as the county success was paralleled by the gestation of another outstanding crop of Bellaghy senior footballers.

They moved impressively through the Derry and Ulster club championships and on to the All-Ireland stage once again. Another national club title proved just beyond them, but with Bellaghy's pre-eminence in Derry circles all but copper-fastened, Seán Brown was at last able to take a step back and realise that his hard work and that of his father before him had been worth it. When his son looks back, he is engulfed by feelings of admiration.

> There is pride because my father oversaw one of the more successful periods in the history of the club. In 1994 they reached that All-Ireland club final and lost to Kilmacud. But that year we won the senior championship, the reserve championship, the reserve league and the Ulster club minor title as well. That was probably the biggest highlight at that stage because, since then, players from that minor team have developed into seniors. At the minute, there are only a couple of clubs in Derry that could beat Bellaghy, even if we're only playing poorly. In the championship we don't give up — there's just a never-say-lose sort of attitude.

Now that his father has gone, these are moments and memories that are frozen forever in time for Seán junior and the rest of the Brown family. The bond he had with his father can never be replaced. They were a good team, a real partnership.

Seán junior knows that they worked together and part of him can't help wondering what they could have achieved for many more years to come. That's what he misses maybe more than anything else — the togetherness and the shared vision.

> His enthusiasm did dip at times when he got fed up with people not doing anything but he would always bounce back up again. It just went like that. When he became Chairman again, it took more effort. Coming up to the day of a match, between the pair of us, we would have spent nearly all our time down at the club. As soon as Daddy got home from work it was down to the club — if the match was that evening, Mammy mightn't have seen him until the next day. The pair of us would have worked together like that, you know, making sure everything was done. He knew he had some things to do and I looked after other things. My Daddy's mentality was always that if they see you working, they'll work as well. And it did happen like that.

Seán Brown junior stops talking. He is looking at a picture of his father hanging on the living-room wall.

*

The night of 12 May 1997 was one just like any other. The Browns — father and son — were taking advantage of the lengthening evenings to get some work done down around the club. Business as usual. A committee meeting had been planned for later but things were running behind schedule. It had been raining most of the evening and that meant the game between Bellaghy and nearby Banagher was late starting. Nobody liked when things ran late, not least Seán Brown himself.

Seán junior had been getting increasingly involved in the running of the club, which meant that he spent a lot of his spare time with his father. They were a good team. But there were outside pressures as well. It was getting near exam time and Seán junior was having to spend more time up in Belfast at university. Of all nights, this was one when he would have preferred everything to be on time. He had a lot on his mind.

> There was to be a club meeting that night but because it was a dirty, wet night, things were running behind schedule. I was at

> the meeting myself but I had to go to college the next day up in Belfast. My exams were coming up at that stage so I went on home early.

Seán Brown waited behind for everything to finish up. Once the meeting was over, he could close up.

The Browns had taken responsibility for closing up the club at night but, rather than having both of them hanging about, they divided up the nights. On this particular evening, the father understood that it was getting late and that his son would have an early start — the exams were important and the club would still be there when they were finished. The simple solution was that he would stay.

> Basically, one or other of us would have locked up. If he had to get home or had to do something, he would have gone on. That night, I had to go home. Some nights, we would both have come out in his car. But I had my own car that night.

The possibility of being watched or coming under attack were not things to which either of them, or anyone else at the club for that matter, had given much thought. There was a palpable sense around this time — 1997 — that the Troubles as people had known them were nearing their end. The various ceasefires were still in place, although some were more rigorously observed than others. The prospect of meaningful talks between all the relevant political groupings inched ever closer; less than a year later, the Good Friday Agreement would be signed.

There were still on-going problems in the village with regard to the issue of loyalist marches but these were events surrounded more by mistrust and suspicion than by actual violence. Although the Bellaghy club rooms had been burnt in the early 1970s, and twice again during the 1980s, the GAA members in the area did not feel under the same immediate threat as they had done just a few years before. If guards had been let down just a little, that was understandable. The tide seemed to be running only one way and the danger of attack or murder seemed to be receding with each passing day.

Seán Brown remembers:

There was no threat at that stage. There was a bad time in the mid-1990s when people were afraid even to go out of their door. But people around the club never thought that we had done anything to warrant it. Maybe with the parade being blocked and re-routed in the town it heightened the tension at the time. I don't know. I just don't know.

In any case, none of that was on the minds of anybody sitting in the Bellaghy club that night. It had been a long evening and the rain hadn't helped things. Most of them were just looking forward to getting home. Seán junior had already left them to it.

The meeting had run on late. The football match had finished at ten o'clock even though the meeting was supposed to be at nine. So they didn't start until ten, and it ran on that bit later and wasn't over till half-eleven. And I suppose there wouldn't be that many people out at half-eleven compared to half-ten. When it gets that bit later, the ones that did it get that bit more confident.

As ever, Seán Brown was the last to leave. He was the man in charge. No one except the killers who were waiting for him at the gate can be sure of what happened next. But Seán junior knew the routine so well and there was no reason to suggest that this night was any different for his father.

The jobs that had to be done — turning off the lights, locking the doors and gates — didn't change. They were the same mundane little things members of the Brown family had been doing at the club for generations. Seán junior talks about it in the measured, knowing way of someone who has gone through the same checklist hundreds of times.

Daddy had come out to the front gate to lock it. The alarm was on. With the heightened trouble we had decided to get lights and put one of those security gates going into the club. But it was rarely used and we never really had occasion to. Daddy had come through the gate and he had parked the car at the side of the road before going back to lock it. That's when they got him. They say there were two or three cars involved. We heard different rumours that it was the LVF and there were ones from Tobermore, Desertmartin, Antrim, Randalstown involved, but there was never anything proved. The police themselves knew who did it but they had no proof. Basically they know who the gunmen are on both sides but they just can't prove it.

After the struggle at the gates, Seán Brown was taken from the club. An hour later, his body was found beside his car around 10 miles away in Randalstown. He had been shot. His son and the rest of the family, meanwhile, were at home. When his father didn't arrive home shortly after him, Seán junior thought that the meeting must have overrun — that was often the way of things. He knew nothing about what had happened until the following morning.

> I was getting ready for bed and I noticed that he hadn't come home. But Mammy sent me on to bed. She sat up all night waiting. She never woke me. Then it wasn't until the next morning that we found out.

*

The impact on the Brown family was devastating. Seán junior likens it to a kind of collective shock from which none of them has fully recovered. The terrible circumstances of the murder make it unlikely that they ever will.

> My mother has still never really got over it and I don't think she will ever. The rest of us are not getting over it but we're coming to terms with it. I know he's not going to come back. I know now that he's in heaven because I know he didn't do anything nasty in his life not to warrant going to heaven. That's how I've coped with it. Some of us have coped with it and some of us haven't really coped with it. It's hitting them hard.

Seán's mother has found the years since her husband's death particularly difficult. Her loss has been acute.

> I know my mother did everything with my father; he took her everywhere with him really. That was ripped away from her and for that simple fact I can't forgive them. I can forgive for some things but not for the way they ripped away her whole sense of belonging from her.

The murder provoked a huge response and a massive outpouring of public sympathy. Seán Brown had touched many lives through his involvement with the sport and the Association he loved. That contribution was reciprocated by the large presence at his funeral. The GAA support structures had kicked in and the family used that as a crutch to help through that difficult period.

> At that stage it did help; it definitely did help. I didn't really feel it as much maybe as the other ones. I didn't care and I just wanted to be left alone. But one night here at the wake there were three Presidents of the GAA in the house — Jack Boothman, Joe McDonagh and Seán McCague — and there were other people who were well-known in GAA circles at the time. That showed to me the sense of esteem in which Daddy was actually held. His name had travelled so far. Daddy had got on so well with each of those people. He approached them in a down-to-earth way and they liked that because they all came from grass-roots level as well.

Seamus Heaney was in Greece at the time of the murder and in a letter to the Belfast newspaper, *The Irish News,* he invoked the spirit of that country to register his disgust at what had happened. The Nobel Laureate wrote:

> Seán Brown's murder was shocking and sinister. I have known two generations of the Brown family. They are people of great probity, much respected in the Bellaghy district, so my heart goes out to them at this moment. I heard the news in Olympia, just after I had visited the stadium where the original Olympic games were held, and given Seán Brown's role as chairman of the Gaelic Athletic Club in Bellaghy, I could not help thinking of his death as a crime against the Olympic spirit.

It was an eloquent and poignantly expressed tribute from one son of Bellaghy to another.

Seán Brown's murder was a crystallisation of the long-running campaign of intimidation and terror against GAA members in the area around Bellaghy. By attacking and killing him, the paramilitaries were showing that the entire Association not only in south Derry but throughout Northern Ireland was still under threat. His son says:

> At that stage, we knew that it was being aimed directly at the GAA in the mid-Ulster area. From Cargin over in Antrim to here, and then sweeping down to the Lough Neagh shore and then back into south Derry. They had come trying to get somebody, and because Bellaghy is the biggest and best-known club in that area, they came here. It was no coincidence. An easy

target. Unless they're very stupid or very brave they don't go after a target that might fire back at them.

Despite the knowledge that Seán Brown's intimate involvement with the GAA led ultimately to his being singled out, the family has no regrets about his devotion and dedication to the Association.

> Put it this way, I'm glad he was involved. It helped him because when I was younger he had no real involvement but when he was asked back again it drove him on and he was proud to represent Bellaghy. And he got me involved — he got all of us involved at some stage. And a lot of the senior players know now that if they had wanted anything, my father would have done his utmost for them. He was that sort of person and they respected him for that.

However, while Seán and the rest of the family have begun to come to terms with the fact of their father's death, they find the fall-out from it difficult to accept. Nobody has ever been convicted of the murder and it seems increasingly unlikely that anyone ever will be.

> My mother looks at this now and sees this whole peace process and thinks it's just a big joke. If they had got anybody, they'd be out now anyway. But the way I look at it is that it would still have been nice to see a conviction for terrorism against a name, because then you haven't got freedom of movement. You mightn't be allowed into certain countries because of it. That's always going to be hanging over you and you're on parole for the rest of your life.

*

Seán Brown junior is an engineer now and works in Belfast. He still lives in the family home and travels part of the same road his father used to back to Bellaghy every evening. After his father's death, he spent a long time considering his relationship with the club. Part of what had made it so worthwhile and vital to him — the intimacy and connection with his father as they worked together — had been taken away from him, and Seán could not see what would replace it.

I did think about leaving. I was close to calling quits at the club convention two years ago because I needed a break from the pressure. I was missing the link with my father. He had been there and if he was there yet I would still have given my time. Whatever he would have done, I would have done.

What he discovered, though, was that the bonds go too deep to sever as easily as that. The ties that bind the Browns to Bellaghy Wolfe Tones go back over sixty years.

I have to say I did look at it all, but I've decided I'm staying in there. I want to ensure that the stuff my father has done around there remains. For a certain period of time, not forever. The club would have been one of my bigger priorities before, but it's well down the list now. Nothing lasts forever.

The scars have barely begun to heal. Bellaghy is still a damaged club and is only taking the first few tentative steps on the long climb back towards normality.

To be honest, they're still recovering. We're in a period of transition. People are still afraid to come around the club. It's the older hands and what we need now is more younger people to drive it forward, people in their forties and fifties.

Seán Brown junior spends just as much time around the club as before, sitting on committees and cajoling people in the same way his father used to. It is painful for him but, at the same time, strangely comforting. The connection is still there.

It's the simple things around here. He made all the signs, he made the flagpoles for the flags of each club who would come. He was involved in making the gates. The first thing I always notice is the bar on the gates going in. And then the security gates going into the social club. He made them. You see so much he was involved in. A lot of very small things that other people mightn't notice, but I notice them.

It is as if something of Seán Brown can now be found in the very fabric of the Bellaghy club — in its very being. That will never disappear. Seán Brown is still there.

Chapter Nine: Journey's End

It is a Friday evening in August, and the rush-hour traffic is edging its way out of Belfast and into the country. Car-loads of people are leaving the city behind for another week and going home to their towns, their parishes, their farms and their families. Progress is slow as the thin line of cars meanders, first past the GAA pitches that skirt the boundary of the M1 motorway and then beyond Milltown Cemetery. Landmarks and history are everywhere you look here.

The pace gradually picks up and the anonymity of the motorway carries people westwards. As Lisburn, Moira and Craigavon recede into the distance, you hit the GAA country of Tyrone. Dungannon first and then, a little further on, set in off the road, there's the ground where Kileshil plays home games. That's where we used to play under-age championship games all those years ago, and where they still play MacRory Cup games today. The fine clubhouse and groomed pitch seem almost out of place, as if they've been transplanted from somewhere much more urban, right to the middle of the rolling Tyrone countryside.

At the Ballygawley roundabout, the journey back really begins. Just a few miles down the road there's the Canavan home-place on the right-hand side. A whole family of footballers — Peter, Pascal, Stephen — grew up in that house and provided a spine for the local Errigal Ciaran club. The signposts on the roadside start to read like a litany of the small, rural clubs where the pulse of the Northern GAA beats strongest. Beragh.

Carrickmore. Names and places that are redolent of a proud, shared history.

Twenty minutes later we're in Omagh. Right in the centre of the town, just beyond the petrol station and the furniture shop, the traffic lights at the right-hand turn for Cookstown are on red. A break in the journey. It is impossible not to allow your gaze to drift just a little to the left, and on to the scarred bomb site at the junction with Market Street. On 15 August 1998, thirty-one people died at and around this corner in a bombing carried out by the Real IRA. The hoardings are up and there are signs that the rebuilding is almost completed. Just across the road they've finished a simple, understated memorial garden. It is a dignified, thoughtful response to the grotesque challenge laid down by the bomb.

There is a peacefulness about this place now. The contorted, twisted images of the amateur video cameras have given way to a more tranquil picture. Omagh is starting to look every inch the small, self-contained rural town it was before the bombers came. The sheer, brutal toll of the deaths and injuries left the people searching for answers. They have reacted in the only way they could — by regrouping and reorganising; establishing a semblance of order out of the chaos; going on.

Yet, the almost suffocating sense of destruction and devastation still lingers.

It seems to take an age, but eventually the filter light turns green and the line of cars swings right. It's a relief to escape, not to have to sit there powerless and have to absorb it all. The proximity of a place of death on such a savage scale is so deeply unsettling that all you want to do is get away as quickly as you can. Remembering — as the people of this community have come to realise over the days and months since the bomb — is the hardest part of all.

There are not many cars on the road in this part of town. Local people tend to avoid the area if they can. Once again, country gradually leaves town behind, and the road to Cookstown takes over. A few miles further on, a minor road veers off to the right towards the small village of Loughmacrory.

This is a place fabled for its production line of top-quality handballers. But tonight the knots of people who are walking up the slope towards the GAA field are here to watch women's Gaelic football.

The crowd that has assembled is the GAA in microcosm. Hard, mountainy men stand stony-faced waiting for the start. Theirs is not the GAA world of corporate boxes, award dinners and sponsorship deals. They are more at home down here in the foothills among their own people. Their quiet enjoyment at occasions like this is the connection they can make with their daughters, their sisters and their neighbours. The club colours are being carried just as they have been carried for generations before. That is something worth celebrating.

The women outnumber the men here tonight. This explosion of women's football and camogie has emboldened them in a way that didn't seem possible even ten years ago. Whereas the public face of the GAA was once predominantly male, women have now taken their place and, in many cases, have taken the lead. The GAA is a richer, brighter place because of this, and can only prosper from a newer, more inclusive approach. That evolution towards modernity is something to be cherished.

The children are a more fitful presence. Nights like this represent a welcome break from routine, and the opportunity is one to be seized. They run around in excited, chattering groups, all but oblivious to the games about to be played. As yet, their connection with this thing called 'The Club' is only vague and barely realised. For now, it represents only a half-understood idea of belonging, of local people coming together in pursuit of some shadowy goals. All they know now are their colours and the pride that flows from wearing their still-too-big replica shirts.

That will change. Their allegiances and connections will harden into something altogether more concrete. The under-12s will blossom into the under-14s, and from there it will be into the minors and the seniors. Eventually they will take their place alongside their mothers and fathers on some sloped terrace somewhere in the county, and there will be a new generation of young people to follow in their wake. History repeats itself.

As they stand together, looking on, the last of the evening sunshine spreads across the pitch. This is GAA country. These are GAA people.

*

It is 11 August 2000. In four days' time the second anniversary of the Omagh bomb will be marked by a few simple ceremonies and many more painful memories. Just a little over a month later, the Coroner's Inquest into the events of two years ago will re-open all the barely healed wounds. The Inquest will be held in a converted hall at Omagh Leisure Centre. It is the same place to which the relatives hurried on the day of the bomb to scour the lists of survivors that had been posted there. If it was all supposed to have got a little easier over time, that hasn't even started to happen yet.

The poignancy of it all is not lost on the men, women and children who have come here tonight. They are drawn mainly from the rural communities of Galbally and Glenelly because their women's football teams are contesting the final of the Tyrone Junior Championship. Tonight marks journey's end. It is the culmination of those first, tentative players' meetings back in the depths of winter, of those training sessions during the freezing evenings of January and February, and of those obstacles that have had to be met and overcome along the way. The prize for the eventual winners tonight is the Brenda Logue Memorial Trophy.

Brenda Logue grew up in Loughmacrory, just a few hundred yards away from this pitch. On that August afternoon in 1998, she was in Omagh, shopping with her mother and her grandmother — a simple family outing. Just after 3 o'clock Brenda was one of the thirty-one people killed in the bomb that exploded on Market Street. She was 17 years old.

This trophy and its celebration of her life were an attempt by the girls who had grown up playing football with Brenda to make something positive come out of the awful tragedy. When they sat down and began to search for an adequate, fitting response, they were initially bereft of ideas. The sheer enormity and the total futility of it all seemed to have strangled the possibility of any reasonable response. The message of the bomb seemed to be that simple humanity no longer had any place. But they kept searching. And eventually they turned to the GAA.

Player and club chairperson Lorraine McAnespie is keeping one eye on the game between Galbally and Glenelly as she explains:

> When the bomb happened, the girls didn't really know what to do. Brenda had such a role in the football club, and football was such a big part of her life that it seemed fitting she would be remembered within football. That's really how it came about.

*

The bombing of Omagh marked the end of many journeys. It signalled for once and for all the futility of acts of violence or savagery in Northern Ireland; it was incontrovertible proof that once such acts were unleashed, they were simply impossible to direct or control. It also had a polarising effect on many of those who had turned half-hearted condemnation of violence on either side of the Northern conflict into an art form. When it came to the deaths of thirty-one men, women, children and unborn babies there was no middle ground. It was something you either supported or you abhorred. There was no room for equivocation, no place for empty words and gestures.

The Omagh bomb also had an epiphanic effect on the GAA and on its perception of its position within Northern Ireland society. Many of those who were killed — in particular, the young teenage victims — had close links with the Association. A trawl through the list of the dead shows that.

Brenda Logue played in goals both for her club side in Loughmacrory and at under-age level with Tyrone. Gareth Conway was a member of the Tattyreagh club in Tyrone; his father had close associations with handball. Jolene Marlow, a 17-year-old student, played camogie and women's football; her father, a publican in the village of Eskra, was Chairman of their local Emmett's club. Kevin Skelton is a referee and GAA official well-known throughout Tyrone; his wife Philomena was killed but he survived. Numerous other relatives of the victims had close associations with the GAA, either as players or supporters.

The rippling effect of the bomb and its aftermath left few people in the town untouched. Among the hundreds injured there were also players and GAA members, including one member of Omagh's senior football team who suffered serious leg injuries. Many of the members of the emergency services and of the hospital staff also had close GAA connections.

The bomb represented a testing and unprecedented challenge to the GAA. Never before during the history of the Troubles had it found itself confronted so starkly and so directly by the sheer grotesqueness of violence in Northern Ireland. There had been murders of individual members, shootings, arson attacks and intimidation over the previous thirty years, but nothing as horrifically brutal as this. The Omagh bomb did not just provoke responses. It demanded them. The GAA stood right in the middle of the biggest single loss of life in Northern Ireland in the course of the Troubles; it had no choice but to position itself firmly behind its suffering members.

The way in which the GAA reacted, first of all in the days immediately after the bombing, and then in the months that followed, provided a revealing insight into the internal workings of the Association and its uncertain view of its own role within the political and cultural life of Northern Ireland. During the long fall-out from 15 August 1998 we were to see the country's biggest sporting organisation at both its best and its worst. That is no criticism of the Association — one of the particularly difficult fall-outs from the bomb in Omagh was the way in which it challenged old positions and established ways of thinking. The GAA and its members were not the only groupings which had to undergo a fundamental re-evaluation in its aftermath.

For generations, the GAA had been part of what could be called the acceptable face of Irish nationalism. Violence was abhorred, and politics was, in the main, avoided. But lurking somewhere in the background there was still the quasi-republican notion that the securing of Irish unity was a matter of time rather than a topic for rational debate. Over the years the GAA had been able to trundle along, with this baggage in tow, but without ever having to ask just why it was carrying it in the first place. Lip service was paid to the Association's nationalist identity, but few, if any, ever bothered to poke around in the darker recesses of what exactly that meant.

The Omagh bomb catapulted all of that out of the shadows. The comfort blanket of nationalism, to which the GAA had clung throughout the Troubles, now had to be cast aside. The old way had been shown to be the wrong way. After Omagh, the GAA — not only in Northern Ireland, but throughout the island — could never be the same again. That could only be a positive thing.

That process of reassessment and self-analysis was, however, for the future. In the shorter term, the Association had to formulate a tenable position and strategy to deal with a catastrophe on this unprecedented scale. The early signs were not auspicious as the organisation fumbled for a response. Mistakes were made, albeit understandable ones in the circumstances.

The immediate GAA reaction to the Omagh bomb was leaden-footed. Offence was caused and the charges of insensitivity laid against the GAA cannot be explained away easily. Despite everything that had happened, the All-Ireland hurling semi-final between Kilkenny and Waterford went ahead in Croke Park in front of 50,856 people just the day after the bomb. There was a minute's silence in memory of those who had died, but, in the context of the carnage of less than twenty-four hours previously, it seemed an ineffectual and inadequate gesture.

Logistically, it would, of course, have been difficult to reschedule such a high-profile occasion in the GAA calendar. However if the Association had tried, with any degree of vigour, the importance of respecting the memory of the dead would have rendered any hurdles surmountable.

Danny Lynch, public relations officer with the GAA, conceded in the days after the Omagh bomb that the Association's management committee had discussed and then decided against postponing the semi-final:

> It would have come up ... but everything was too advanced. Teams would have been almost on their way, supporters were staying in town. It wouldn't have been feasible.

However, by 6 p.m. on the Saturday, almost twenty-four hours before the hurling semi-final was due to start, twenty-one people had already been confirmed dead, with countless others injured. The decision not to opt for postponement and the justifications given for that decision didn't wash then with the people of Northern Ireland, and they don't wash with them more than two years down the line.

The course of action adopted by the Croke Park hierarchy is thrown into sharp relief by the responses of others, including those from within their own Association. The officials of the Tyrone county board were able to move sufficiently quickly to postpone a senior championship match later that same Saturday evening and to put on hold until further notice all fixtures within Tyrone.

The reactions of other sporting bodies in Northern Ireland also cast the GAA's approach in an unfavourable light. An international football friendly between Northern Ireland and Malta, fixed for the following Wednesday, was swiftly cancelled. 'Football would be totally inappropriate,' said the President of the Irish Football Association, Jim Boyce, as he made the announcement. 'We had no hesitation making the decision.'

Lawrie McMenemy, the then manager of the Northern Ireland side, although a man who would not be expected to have an intimate feel for the place, also struck the right chord:

> It wasn't right to play. A match is a place to go to celebrate. I cannot see anything to celebrate this week.

It is not hard to imagine the overwhelmingly positive impact of these same words had they come from the mouth of a high-ranking GAA official around this time.

Why then was the GAA left so badly exposed and seemingly out of step? Granted, the timescale involved was incredibly short, and the upheaval of moving to postpone the game would have been considerable. But these problems should not have been beyond the scope of a body with the GAA's organisational prowess. Given that the capability must have been there, the inescapable conclusion is that it had much to do with an underlying mind-set.

Deep below the surface of the decision that was made on that Saturday evening was a value system that has characterised the GAA attitude towards events in Northern Ireland for a generation. The substance of that value system and that mind-set is that the GAA in Northern Ireland stands separated and apart from the core of the Association and its decision-making bodies in Dublin. It is partition, GAA style. The Association may not formally recognise the border between Northern Ireland and the Republic but the message that rings loud and clear is that the most significant divisions of all are mental, not physical.

The element of geographical separation, emphasised by the presence of the border, is the obvious physical manifestation of partition. But there is much more to it. During the early period of the Troubles in particular, the murderous violence in Northern Ireland presented so many difficulties for the GAA from both a political and a cultural point of view that it became easier to stand on the outside looking in. Life 'there' — and that included GAA life — was deemed different, unusual and separate.

This had two effects. The GAA, for its part, disengaged from life in Northern Ireland, and it was left to officials on the ground to hold the Association together in the face of considerable political pressure from the rank-and-file members. And, in direct response to that, those same members developed a wariness of the wider GAA family — a wariness fuelled by the suspicion that they had been abandoned to the vagaries of the society that had been erected around them.

Thus, there was a detachment in the way in which the wider GAA community addressed Northern Irish issues during the three decades of the Troubles. Even after the Association had begun to find its voice, words were not backed up by actions. At

Annual Congress, motions condemning the occupation of the Crossmaglen club by the British Army were resoundingly endorsed. When players were singled out for violence, or clubs were subjected to sectarian-fuelled arson attacks, there was full-throated, unequivocal condemnation. There is no doubt that these expressions of disapproval were prompted by noble notions of sympathy and concern. There were good men and women within the GAA in the Republic who were genuinely horrified and disgusted by what was being visited on the Association just a hundred miles away. But their sympathy alone was of limited value when set against the hard currency of Northern Irish political debate.

The extent to which any of these fine, well-intentioned words ever amounted to more than lip-service is a moot point, because none of the worthy gestures was accompanied by the level of real engagement that might have been expected and would certainly have been required. The GAA had discovered the potency of words without action.

However, all of these situations with which the GAA had found itself confronted were as nothing when it came to the human disaster that was the Omagh bomb. One of the many effects of the bomb was to box the GAA into something of a corner, from where it was forced to come up with a whole new set of responses for an unprecedented situation. The way in which it did just that has had both a chastening and an enervating effect on the entire Association. GAA land is ultimately a better place because of it.

*

Brenda Logue was an ebullient character — full of life, everyone says. Every team has its life-force, its inspiration, and for the St Theresa's club, that was Brenda. St Theresa's had only been in existence for three years when she died, but already Gaelic football had become the focal point of her life. Everything began and ended with the football team, and anyone who came into contact with Brenda could not avoid being swept along by her enthusiasm. She was an exciting person to be around.

Mary Connolly is the chair of the women's football county board in Tyrone and, as she stands behind one of the dug-outs watching the final that is being played in Brenda Logue's memory, she is talking about the first time she met her. The memories bring smiles. Memories of Brenda always seem to bring smiles here.

> I met her out one night and she jumped in front of me and said: 'You don't know me but I know you. You're Mary Connolly.' I said: 'That's right. Who are you?' 'I'm Brenda Logue,' she said back to me.

Even before they began organising women's football properly in Loughmacrory, Brenda Logue had set down her marker. If there was going to be any football played in the area, she was going to be involved. That was clear from a very early stage. Timing was on her side because some of the old boundaries within the GAA were already starting to break down. Organised games of football, and training sessions for girls and women, unheard of just a decade before, were becoming part of the fabric of many clubs. Brenda was one of the first to take full advantage. According to Kathleen Conway, secretary of the St Theresa's club:

> She was football-mad. She would have gone to all the football that was put on here at the field, for both the men and the women. She lived over there in the housing estate and she would have been playing about with the boys all the time. And when the men would be over here training, she'd be over as well. She was very lively, full of life, great. She was the life and soul of the club.

They don't talk much about how they miss her. They don't have to.

For someone like that there was really only one position to play — the one place where you could almost guarantee to be at the centre of all the action. Goalkeeper. There was nowhere else for a show-off and an exhibitionist. So Brenda Logue became a goalkeeper. Kathleen Conway remembers:

> She was involved right from the start, and she would have been one of the better players. She finished up as a goalkeeper and she was a very good goalkeeper.

And if things got a little excited now and again, there wasn't too much of a fuss made. Brenda had already stamped her character all over the club. Kathleen Conway laughs fondly at the thought of it all. The affection cannot be disguised. 'She would get into the odd scrimmage too. Nothing too serious. It was all in the good cause of the club.'

For a few of the local girls the football team had been something of a nine-day wonder. After the initial flushes of enthusiasm, numbers began to ebb away. But Brenda was in for the long haul. Kathleen Conway says:

> The first night we started, we had a meeting down in the hall and there was a great turnout. Registration was a fiver and I think at the end of the night we had something like £500. Two of the men agreed to coach the team — you know, to start them off. They did very well with them because there was a lot of them hadn't a clue. They didn't even know how to line up, that sort of thing, who to mark, where to stand.

Every new venture needs its unshakeable advocates and Brenda Logue was more than happy to fill that role. Her exuberance carried some of her more reluctant team-mates along, almost despite themselves. Lorraine McAnespie recalls:

> Brenda really enjoyed her football; she was definitely a backbone to the team. She was always the one who would be there enjoying the crack, messing about, you know. She enjoyed the training as well, which I suppose would be unusual. It would be her who would be dragging them all over to train. If she saw some of them hanging around who weren't coming to training, she'd take them over. She was so involved, and when she got on to the county team it was such a big thing for her.

Tyrone. It meant so much to Brenda. Playing for your club was a great thing, lining out alongside your friends and your neighbours. But the county was a different thing altogether. This was where the real action was, and it was where Brenda Logue wanted to be — right there in the middle of it all. That county career had just started before the bomb, as Brenda made the under-16 Tyrone team. With women's football within Tyrone on an upward turn, the next target in her sights would have been the senior team and the chance to play in some of the more famous GAA venues. It never looked like she would be content to settle for second-best.

All that optimism, all those longed-for big occasions disappeared with the bomb. The village of Loughmacrory and the St Theresa's club were left totally bereft. The days after the bomb, with the funerals and the slow climb back towards some normality, had a dreadfully traumatic effect on the club and the girls who had played alongside Brenda. She had died towards the end of the summer and the end of the football season. Now even the most mundane team activities and responsibilities carried their own searing pain.

It fell to people like Kathleen Conway to pull together a group which looked like it might disintegrate under the sheer weight of it all, and splinter in a thousand different directions. She remembers:

> We had one more game to play in the League after that, after she died. We dragged it on for a bit but we just had to play that game because I don't think we would have had a team again if we hadn't gone out that year and played it.

There were times when they thought it was just going to be too much to bear. Somehow, though, they dragged themselves together and regrouped. The shared strength was all they had left.

> It was very hard. The girl who did goals had to take Brenda's place. It was very tough for her. The game we had to play was against Strabane in Drumquin about six or seven weeks after the bomb. Now, they just didn't want to play and I said to them: 'Girls, we have to play, we have to go out and play this game.' And they did go out and they did it. The Strabane girls were very good to them too. It was just very emotional.

They got through. Somehow they got through.

*

The poignancy and symbolism of the bombing of Omagh operate on myriad different levels. The degrees of grief and suffering are amplified by the fact that the death toll included young and old, Protestant and Catholic, Gaelic footballers and rugby players, town people and country people, Irish and Spanish. This was an act of violence that was indiscriminate to the point of barbarity.

More than any single terrorist incident in the history of the Troubles, the Omagh bomb was an atrocity that cut a swathe through the traditional boundaries. No one side had a monopoly on either grief or condemnation. The pain was evenly spread out and commonly shared. None of the old rules of engagement which dictated how one community or another would react to a particular incident could be applied. Everyone had simply to start again.

Among the GAA members who died, there were signs of the new order that was emerging within its own ranks as well. The most vibrant section of the GAA community in the past decade has been the growing group of camogie players and women's Gaelic footballers. Ulster has been one of the fulcrums of this explosion of interest, with new clubs catering for the interests of women within the GAA mushrooming all over the province.

Brenda Logue was part of that revolution. When women's Gaelic football began to cut the apron strings from its male big brother, Brenda Logue seized on the new opportunities it offered. And as the game began to move ever more confidently centre stage, Brenda went enthusiastically with the flow. Again, the old rules did not apply and Brenda and many like her revelled in the freedom. After years of being hidebound by the time-worn old strictures, women within the GAA now had the chance to soar.

Just a few miles across Tyrone in Eskra, Jolene Marlow had been making the same journey. She was a member of the St MacCartan's women's team in nearby Augher, and just ten days before the bomb in Omagh she had been part of the side that won a Tyrone championship. At her funeral, a guard of honour was formed from young people in the local GAA community, including the Eskra Emmett's camogie team.

Brenda and Jolene were young members of a GAA that was undergoing a period of fundamental change. A new generation had been emerging, and they were both part of it. Brenda and Jolene could participate actively within the Association at a level women of just one generation before would not have imagined possible. Women had got involved in officialdom in some counties, even as far as county board level, but they were rarities. And, in any case, this was different — Brenda realised that when she used to hang around watching the boys and the men out playing on Loughmacrory's pitch. Playing was the thing, all that mattered — the real GAA.

For a century, the GAA had remained resolutely male and patriarchal and had clearly begun to stagnate as a result. There had been some tentative stirrings before the women's revolution. During the 1990s some of the reforms to the hurling championship breathed new life into a structure that had become stale and predictable. Football, meanwhile, was struggling to keep up, but had instead regressed to a version of the game which valued the creation of a production line of muscle-bound automatons over the lithe unpredictability of skill and intermittent sprinklings of genius. It was slowly and inexorably becoming a game that was having all the humanity choked out of it.

Before the invigoration it received from the prodigious growth of the women's game, Gaelic football was all but out on its feet, punch-drunk after years of valuing results over technique. But women like Brenda Logue, Jolene Marlow and the countless others who were now playing the game at club and colleges level saved it from itself. The obvious physical disadvantages that women faced were turned into positions of strength, as increased emphasis was placed on the virtues of ball skills and accurate passing. There are times now when watching a game of women's football is eerily reminiscent of the way in which the men's game was played thirty or forty years ago. That has been one of its greatest contributions. Modern women's football is a reminder of what has been lost.

The GAA had also been offered a glimpse of how its future could be, and that future was female as well as male. It was a way of getting back in touch with some of the core values and founding principles. So the Omagh bomb and the deaths of women like Brenda Logue and Jolene Marlow was not just an attack on the GAA of the present. It also stripped it of part of its future.

Nevertheless, there is optimism about what lies ahead. The confidence of the women who helped football bed down in Loughmacrory was shaken in the aftermath of the Omagh bomb but the roots were sturdy enough to support new growth. Lorraine McAnespie says:

> I think it's good that women can now get involved in the GAA. I think people's attitudes are definitely changing as well. You can see from the support here tonight, lots of men and women here together. They see women's football as good sport in itself.

There is also enough self-assurance to keep pushing out the boundaries and to continue asking hard questions of some of the more reluctant GAA mandarins.

> Club-wise, I suppose it can only get stronger, and, county-wise, it will go from strength to strength with the likes of Monaghan and Tyrone going so well here in Ulster. Getting more of our games on with the men would definitely be a big plus. The media coverage has been important because girls watch it on television and think: 'God I could do that — that's something I might be good at or interested in.'

*

However unwelcome and unwanted it may have been, the GAA found the spotlight turned back on itself. There had been murders of its members and attacks on its premises at numerous points throughout the Troubles, and the Association had had to mourn its dead and care for its injured. But the effect of the bombing of Omagh was fundamentally different. First of all, there was the youth of those who died — Brenda Logue and Jolene Marlow were 17, Gareth Conway was 18. Then there was the way in which it cut across any of the old, traditional gender barriers that used to define the Association. The GAA as a body was already in the process of making itself more contemporary. The impact of those early, green shoots of reform were there for all to see in the lives of those who died.

The GAA was both confronted and confused by the Omagh bomb — its biggest crisis of the Troubles. Instead of taking up its customary position on the margins, it was hurled into the unforgiving glare of the spotlight. Its reaction in the first twenty-four hours was the first major test and it made the hasty decision to go ahead with the All-Ireland hurling semi-final the following day. These were shaky, uncertain times.

As the weekend blurred into the new week, the emergence of every little private detail about each of the victims personalised the tragedy of Omagh. Instead of a collective death toll of thirty-one victims, there were now thirty-one poignant stories, each of which stood alone as indictments of the inhumanity of what had been done.

Brenda Logue, Jolene Marlow and Gareth Conway had all been looking to the future. Brenda had sat her GCSEs during the summer. Jolene was hoping her A-level results would get her into a physiotherapy course at the University of Ulster. Gareth had already been accepted for an engineering course at Magee College. The results of the exams which Brenda and Jolene had sat arrived at their homes as their families were preparing for their funerals.

For the families the funerals were unbearably sad occasions, but for others the ceremony and the very public displays of sympathy were also a means of beginning the process of coming to terms with what had happened, not just to the dead and their relatives but also to the wider community.

There were countless simple but important gestures. Eight-year-old Oran Doherty was a Celtic fanatic and he was buried with a club shirt draping his coffin. Celtic were represented at his funeral in Buncrana by Marc Reiper, then a Danish international centre-half, and Willie McStay, the youth team coach. Reiper is a mountain of a man, and the picture of him balancing the small, child-sized coffin on one huge shoulder is one of the enduring images of those traumatic days after the bombing. When the then Leeds United manager, George Graham, was told that one of the injured was a Leeds supporter, he travelled to the Erne Hospital in Enniskillen to meet him.

After the hesitancy and uncertainties of its initial response, the GAA was not found wanting amidst all this selflessness and goodness. As the terrible cycle of funerals began on the Tuesday after the bomb, Joe McDonagh, the president of the Association, made the short, sad criss-cross journeys across Tyrone from one funeral to another. The timings of some had been staggered so that mourners could attend as many as possible. McDonagh stood shoulder to shoulder with people at as many as he could.

In graveyards in Drumquin, Eskra and Carrickmore, McDonagh and countless other GAA people from county board level right down to the humblest of club members came together in acts of collective respect. At Philomena Skelton's funeral in Drumquin there wasn't enough room around the small plot for all the people who had turned up. And there, right in the centre, was the GAA president, shaking hands, talking to people, and providing leadership in the truest sense of the word.

It was not the sort of leadership that makes fine, thundering speeches at Congress. Nor was it the sort of leadership that sits at the head of committees in Croke Park adjudicating on this suspension or that appeal. Nor the sort of leadership that cuts ribbons to open new, multi-million pound stands. Nor yet the sort of leadership that tries to keep an amateur finger in the dyke as the tide of professionalism threatens to wash over the top. This was real leadership — leadership from the heart and from the very soul of the GAA.

Joe McDonagh's presidency may have had turbulent times, but he injected vibrancy and a sense of well-being into the entire Association. Just a few months before Omagh he had misjudged the Ulster mood with his ill-advised attempt to rush through the removal of Rule 21 from the GAA rule-book. But in the days after the bomb he was perfectly in tune with the GAA mood and did all that could have been expected of him.

However, nothing Joe McDonagh did or said at any other time during his presidency comes close to matching the importance of his presence at those GAA funerals that followed the Omagh bomb. In the years and decades to come, that humanity and that willingness to prove to the GAA people of Tyrone that they were not alone and that they had no reason to feel isolated by what had happened to them, will stand as his towering, lasting achievement. It was a sign that the GAA could function in reality as the coherent, one-nation unit it had always been in theory. It was journey's end.

Nevertheless, the GAA still found the construction of a coherent and consistent response to the tragedy of Omagh problematic. Its approach remained bedevilled by contradictions as the fall-out continued. First, there was the public relations disaster concerning the use of the principal GAA pitch in the town, Healy Park, as the venue for three fund-raising games against teams from the English Premiership.

Manchester United, Chelsea and Liverpool had agreed to come to Omagh to help the appeal fund that had been set up in the wake of the bomb. Concerned that the limited capacity of Omagh Town's St Julian's Road ground would affect adversely the amount of money that could be raised, the club's manager, Roy McCreadie, approached the GAA for help. Healy Park had recently been renovated to Ulster Championship standard and could hold perhaps three times as many fans as St Julian's Road.

The appetite for the games and the goodwill of people throughout the country were already in place, and this seemed like a pragmatic solution to a difficult situation. Given that the ultimate and only beneficiary of all of this would be the bomb fund, there seemed little problem. But that was where the GAA rule-book kicked in. A ground operated under the auspices of the Association could not be used for a game in another code such as soccer without an express change to that rule-book.

When this entire issue was catapulted into the newspaper and television headlines in September 1998, the GAA used the need for this rule change as the justification for its refusal to sanction the use of Healy Park, and showed no apparent willingness to usher through such a change to facilitate the playing of the games. The media squall continued but the GAA stood firm. When the fund-raising games were eventually played in autumn 1999, it was at St Julian's Road. The GAA had shown itself not to be for turning.

However one chooses to look at it, the inescapable truth is that the GAA's obstinate refusal to allow its ground to be used was, in all the circumstances, the wrong thing to do. But, the GAA being the GAA, the situation did not remain as clear-cut or as black-and-white as that for too long.

The GAA engaged in its own drive to raise money for the Omagh appeal, and channelled gate receipts and other revenue into its own fund. This turned out be more than a casual gesture because the GAA subsequently emerged as the single biggest contributor to the appeal fund. In May 2000, Joe McDonagh, the Association president, Liam Mulvihill and officials from the Tyrone and Donegal county boards gathered at Healy Park in Omagh to present a cheque for £750,000 to the trustees of the appeal. Even the choice of venue was laced with typical GAA irony, but there was no escaping the enormity of the contribution. The GAA had delivered.

The entire Healy Park saga with the final dénouement of the £750,000 contribution provides a telling snapshot of the GAA and all its magnificent contradictions. The events as they unfolded cast it first in an uncaring, unresponsive light, but then, just a little way down the road, the Association displayed its credentials as a compassionate, caring, selfless organisation.

*

Brenda Logue's friends and team-mates were at her funeral. They helped put a St Theresa's shirt on the coffin, and they stood in silent tribute to her and to her memory. That helped. Her life and her death had been marked and they had been there to be a part of that.

However, as the days after the bomb turned into weeks, it became obvious to a lot of them that it wasn't going to be enough. Brenda had been such a part of the life of the club and the lives of the women she played alongside. Somewhere deep down, they knew that there was something missing. The circle of her death and everything that there was to celebrate in her life had not been completed.

Bit by bit they went through that process. First they went to Kathleen Conway, the secretary of the club, and together they came up with the idea of buying a plaque for Brenda's grave. Now there was something that would last — something permanent that would tell the story of Brenda and her GAA life. But still they searched for a way of making a more intimate and enduring connection with the GAA. It had to be intertwined with the future of women's football in Tyrone. Kathleen Conway says:

> We had lost Brenda and we had lost our goalie. The year she died there was no junior championship but at the end of that year the girls were keen to do something to remember Brenda by. They bought the plaque for her grave and then they said could we not buy a cup and maybe the county board would use it then for some competition.

Everything had started to fall into place. The women's game in Tyrone was expanding rapidly and the time had come to initiate a junior competition for those teams just starting out and those who had fallen on harder times after a period in the higher divisions. Mary Connolly and the rest of the Tyrone women's county board realised that it was the perfect opportunity to commemorate Brenda's death with a competition in her name that was proof of the prodigious growth of the sport she had loved.

> After the bomb, the Loughmacrory club asked could they sponsor a trophy. At that stage we had only two championships and we weren't sure where we were going to put the cup. But there were more clubs joining at the time so we decided we'd make a third league and then, therefore, a junior championship. Up until then it had been just junior and senior but we added an intermediate league.

The county board had felt the same nagging compulsion to act as Brenda's Loughmacrory team-mates, and now a perfect opportunity had presented itself.

According to Mary Connolly:

> Brenda had been so closely involved in Loughmacrory and then with the county under-16 team. It was a nice thing to be able to do and then the St MacCartan's club sponsored a club-of-the-year trophy in memory of Jolene Marlow. So we now have that at the end of the year as well.

With a remarkable symmetry, the three clubs in Tyrone who had lost young players turned to the GAA for suitable tributes. Gareth Conway's Tattyreagh club inaugurated an inter-club tournament in his name, which has now become an annual fixture. The dovetailing of the awards and tributes — the Jolene Marlow club-of-the-year award, the Brenda Logue memorial trophy and the Gareth Conway tournament — could not have been more apposite or more fitting. As long as men's and women's Gaelic football continues to be played in Tyrone and Ulster, their names will be forever to linked to it. In years to come, after the painful vividness of the memories of Omagh has begun to soften just a little around the edges, they will be remembered. And the GAA will always be an intrinsic part of that process of collective memory.

By the beginning of the 1999 season, one year after the bomb, GAA life in Northern Ireland had begun to return to some semblance of normality. There was no forgetting, but there was also no standing still. The training sessions began again and the competition of the league and the championship became something to look forward to. Events then took on a life of their own. What followed was the best tribute that could be imagined to the life of Brenda Logue.

After the aching experiences of Brenda's death and funeral, her team-mates had already had to endure the trauma of fulfilling their last league game of the 1998 season against Strabane. Together they got through that. By the start of the following year, they had regrouped and, bit by bit, things started to fall into place. The St Theresa's club now found itself in the new junior division. According to Kathleen Conway:

> Numbers had already started to fall away a bit, and the older ones were getting fed up because they weren't winning anything. Then when the junior section was formed, that was right into our pocket because we would have been one of the stronger junior teams.

Loughmacrory performed well right through the junior league and won it with something to spare. But somewhere at the back of their collective consciousness there was the championship — Brenda's championship. That became the focus and the goal. Lorraine McAnespie says:

> I suppose the championship in itself was a good thing to aim for and then when it was named after Brenda that gave the girls something extra to be aiming towards.

One year after the Omagh bomb, St Theresa's won that junior championship. Of all the tributes that had been paid and the mourning that had been done, this was the one that towered over all the others. It had been for Brenda. Kathleen Conway will never forget the occasion or the feeling.

> When we came home with the cup that night, it was very emotional. It was just so great for us to win that. The hairs are standing on the back of my neck even now just thinking about it. We knew we had a chance and the girls just had it in their heads that we were going to win that cup. That's what kept them going last year. Even tonight when we were organising this final, some of the girls were asking me if this had been done for them last year. And it had. They were that proud and that happy about winning and still are.

Lorraine McAnespie believed it was an act of closure and a way in which the club could find it within itself to move forward out of the darkness.

> It definitely was so emotional. They were really delighted because they went out to win it for Brenda, and all they wanted to do was to bring the cup which was named after her back home. And that's what they managed to do. I think we all felt we were doing something for her.

It had taken a year, but St Theresa's too had reached the end of its journey. It had begun with a traumatic loss, but the players and the officials used the GAA as a means of finding a way through it. The long hours of preparation for the championship, the training, the tactics had become a way of coping. To win the championship and the Brenda Logue memorial trophy that went with it was the closure they all needed — never forgetting, but leaving some of the terrible pain in the past.

*

After a nervous start, the favourites, Galbally Oonagh Celts have beaten Glenelly 5–13 to 2–4 to become the second winners of the Tyrone junior championship named in Brenda Logue's honour. That trophy will be leaving Loughmacrory now as the people of Galbally carry it away in triumph, but there is not even the slightest hint of regret about that. It has done its cathartic work.

In the gathering gloom of the evening, the impromptu presentation ceremony begins. The Galbally players hug each other and chatter excitedly, while the beaten Glenelly team stand in small, disappointed groups, eager for it all to be over so that they can escape to the dressing rooms. A makeshift public address system has been rigged up, but Mary Connolly struggles to be heard above the intermittent Galbally celebrations. She congratulates the new champions but makes especially sure to pay tribute to the young and inexperienced Glenelly team. Women's football in Tyrone needs all the new blood it can get.

There is something reassuringly familiar about all of this, something comforting about being part of the same GAA continuum of winners and losers, of hopes and disappointments that has been turning for over a century. The whole scene is subsumed by an unspoken sense of belonging, of being part of the GAA family. These are GAA people.

When the speeches have finished, the Galbally captain, Colleen Quinn, comes forward to accept the junior championship cup. Brenda Logue's mother waits for her. The trophy named after her daughter is gripped tightly between her hands. She looks just a little ill at ease in front of all these people and the newspaper cameras. Hers is an ordinary life made extraordinary by what happened to Brenda during that shopping trip to Omagh almost two years before. But she is here and the Logue family is doing the best it can.

When the presentation finishes, the crowds stream away and the car park empties as the journeys back home begin. The players make their way to the dressing rooms, some stopping to talk to relatives and friends who wandered over to find them. Another year's football is over but this is not the end. This is never the end. Already some minds are turning to next year and how it might all be so different. The great imponderables. But they will all be back because the GAA has them now. It is part of their very being.

*

Later, on the car radio there is a report from Derry about the search for a suspected Real IRA car bomb. The newsreader says it seems to have been intended for the city centre. I think about Brenda Logue and her short, GAA-filled life. I think about all the experiences she will never have, all the games in which she will never play. And I think about a mother losing her daughter and standing at the side of a football field, nervously clasping the trophy which now bears her name. This is what it is all ultimately reduced to. This is the image everyone should see.

After that, there is no going back. There can be no going back.